STEM Secrets
The X-Factor of Leadership
Harnessing the Power of Respectful Leadership
Jeffrey Harvey P.E.

Apollo Digital Group LLC

COPYRIGHT

ISBN: 979-8-9866340-5-0 (ebook)
ISBN: 979-8-9866340-6-7 (pbk)
Publisher: Apollo Digital Group LLC, Wyoming
Website: www.jeffreyharveype.com

Contents

Are you looking to take the next step in your leadership journey?

Free Giveaways

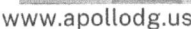

Introduction

From Aspiration to Action: The Journey to Becoming a Respected and Effective Leader

A leader is best when people barely know he exists, when his work is done, his aim fulfilled, they will say: we did it ourselves. – Lao Tzu

Leadership is a critical aspect of any organization as it determines the direction, vision, and success of the company. In today's fast-paced and rapidly changing business environment, it has become increasingly important for leaders to possess a range of skills and qualities that enable them to navigate through uncertainty, adapt to change, and drive progress.

The aim of this book is to provide readers with an in-depth understanding of the qualities and skills that are critical to effective leadership in today's business world. Through a combination of research, case studies, and practical examples, this book will explore the nine key qualities that define highly respected leaders. These qualities include integrity, strong communication skills, vision, self-awareness, emotional intelligence, decisiveness, empowerment, and adaptability.

Each chapter of this book will delve into one of these qualities, examining what each quality means, why it is important, and how it can be developed and honed. Moreover, the book will provide practical examples of leaders who possess these qualities and explore the impact they have had on their organizations and teams.

In addition to exploring the nine key qualities of highly respected leaders, this book will also offer readers tips and tools for developing these qualities within themselves. Whether you are an aspiring leader, an experienced manager, or simply someone who is interested in personal and professional development, this book will provide you with the knowledge and guidance you need to enhance your leadership skills.

The book will also explore the role of leadership in creating a positive, productive, and empowering workplace culture. It will examine the impact of leadership on team morale, employee engagement, and overall organizational success, as well as offer readers practical strategies for fostering a culture of trust, respect, and collaboration.

Whether you are looking to advance your career, start a new business, or simply improve your leadership skills, this book is an invaluable resource. With its comprehensive and practical approach, it will provide you with the knowledge and tools you need to become a more effective, confident, and respected leader.

Overall, this book is a must-read for anyone interested in understanding the qualities and skills that define highly respected leaders and developing these qualities within themselves. Supported by research, practical examples, and expert advice, it provides a comprehensive and accessible guide to leadership in today's business world.

What Sparked My Interest in Writing This Book?

As a new career leader, I found myself constantly helping my team solve problems. Although my intentions were good, as they were centered around making my team more effective, they were sometimes interpreted as micromanagement. Sadly, I kept making similar mistakes as I moved up the ranks. While I was considered a great problem solver and analytical thinker by my leaders, those I led didn't always welcome my approach.

However, I was fortunate enough to work with leaders who helped me identify my weaknesses and taught me how to be a more effective leader. I have always had a very technical mind and conducted myself with integrity, but when it came to giving my team the autonomy they needed to grow and take the initiative, I was always found wanting. My technical mind proved to be a blessing and a curse—a blessing in that I was always able to identify problems or possible problems and solve them, and a curse in that I hardly gave my team a chance to express themselves, show initiative, and grow in their respective fields. To be honest, it was my way or the highway, and as a result, I often dismissed my team's ideas and opinions. Although I am making progress in rectifying this behavior, I still struggle with it at times.

I have learned to brainstorm and poke holes in different areas with my team. I also allow them to brainstorm among themselves in order to find the best solution for a problem. This allows them to be creative and come up with improved or different solutions. I only intervene when there's a fatal flaw in their solution, and instead of telling them what to do, I ask them questions to get a sense of why they came up with that solution. I also give them room to dig deeper into their suggested solution before I proceed with their recommendations.

Moreover, after lots of work and research, I have now adopted a value-based leadership style. This type of leadership is when leaders consider their own core values and those defined by the work organization for motivation and guidance. While this leadership style has many strengths, it comes with its fair share of weaknesses. Without diving into either the strengths or weaknesses at this point, I must say that I was triggered or unimpressed when people failed to follow corporate rules, focus on impact, help others, or overall lacked integrity. Consequently, my response to these issues was disproportionate compared to when I knew someone made an honest mistake with similar outcomes. When the issues involved honest mistakes, I was more forgiving.

My association with other leaders or business partners with different leadership styles helped me put things into proportion. I started asking them if the position I wanted to take on certain issues seemed reasonable or if they had a different idea of how to approach it. This helped me balance my response to individuals and allowed me to take a breath when I hit one of my triggers.

My company would do corporate surveys, which allowed staff members to rate their direct and executive leader's leadership styles, and as I continued to work on my reaction to triggers and improve my overall approach to leadership, I began to see my leadership scores increase. Before I knew it, my ratings were getting closer to the top, and while I knew I still had a lot of improvements to make, being aware of my triggers and understanding my leadership style helped me to improve and not only become an effective leader, but a highly respected one.

Dear Leaders, it's time to evaluate your leadership style and take it to the next level. I urge you to keep reading this and reflect on how you can implement the insights it provides. By learning and honing these qualities, you can become a better leader, earn the respect of your team, and drive success for your organization. Don't wait any longer; take action today to improve your leadership skills and make a positive impact on your team and organization!

Chapter 1

Great Leaders Have Integrity

The greatness of a man is not in how much wealth he acquires, but in his integrity and his ability to affect those around him positively. – Bob Marley

No one can claim to be a highly respected leader without integrity. You can instill fear in your team and get things done, but to earn their respect, you need to have integrity. One can even suggest or put forward that it's the most vital quality for effective leadership. This is because it sets the tone for the actions and decisions you make as a leader. Integrity is often defined as being honest and having strong moral principles, both of which are crucial components of a leader's character. Nothing inspires trust and confidence in your team more than demonstrating integrity at all times, and as if that's not enough, you get to foster a culture of ethics and accountability. Simply put, having integrity means that you will be transparent in your communications, dedicated to following through on your commitments, and fair in your decision-making.

Moreover, leaders with integrity are not too proud to admit when they're wrong or take responsibility for their actions. They avoid taking part in unethical or illegal practices and make it a point to always be a good representative of their team, stakeholders, and organization. Because they strive to create a culture of trust and respect, leaders with integrity go beyond talking the talk as they work every day to model the morals and standards they set for their teams. In today's fast-paced and increasingly complex business environment, integrity is more important than ever as it helps leaders to navigate challenging situations and maintain the trust of their stakeholders. Eventually, a leader's integrity is a reflection of their character and is essential for building strong and successful organizations.

Seven Principles to Help You Achieve Leadership Integrity

When you have integrity, your actions match your words, you honor your commitments, and you model the values you try to instill in your team. Sometimes leaders take advantage of their position, and instead of abiding by the code of conduct, they break the rules. While there are different provisions in each organization's code of conduct, there are some common ones across the business world. These include workplace harassment, fair treatment of staff, privacy and confidentiality, and accuracy of corporate finances, to mention a few. However, whether leaders realize this or not, effective leadership is not attainable without their team's trust. When teams question their leader's standards or integrity, trust can never be achieved. According to recent Gallup surveys, employees in Europe and the United States do not trust their leaders. This is mainly because employees fail to understand what their leaders believe, which points to a communication problem between management and staff (Todorovic, n.d.).

Sadly, the reality of business is that if relationships are not based on trust, production and quality of work can be negatively affected. This lack of trust that stems from a lack of integrity by leaders does not only affect them at a personal or business level, but it affects the business as a whole.

You may be wondering if you have been leading with integrity, and to help you reach your own conclusion, here are a few questions you can ask yourself:

- Am I respected for my actions?

- Do I hold myself accountable for my decisions?

- Am I a good role model for my team?

- Do my actions match my words?

- Do I follow through on my promises and commitments?

If the answer to all these questions is not a strong yes, or if you doubt your integrity, there's always room for improvement. While there are many ways to display integrity, here are some of the most profound principles to help you get there (Nadler, n.d.):

Build a Good Reputation

Building a good reputation when you're a leader is very vital. This is because leaders represent the company, and should their reputation be tarnished, it affects the entire organization. When building a good reputation, you should take a holistic approach to it. That means that while your work should be top-tier, the way you relate with and treat those subordinate to you, and those in higher positions than you should also be exemplary. It's not complicated; consistent honesty, responsibility, and reliability will do the trick. You should also remember that while building a good reputation takes a lifetime, you can destroy it in one moment. Therefore, it's crucial to always model the right behavior in and outside your work.

Maintain High Moral Standards

Maintaining high moral standards goes hand in hand with building a good reputation—one can't thrive without the other. As a leader, having high moral standards will stop you from questionable practices and behaviors like cutting corners, accepting bribes, and being the perpetrator of sexual harassment. Not only will you model good behavior for your team, but you will earn their trust.

Honor Your Commitments

Without a doubt, the commitments you make can directly impact your integrity. Do you want to be known as someone who does not honor their word or as a reliable leader? The choice is yours, but if you choose the latter, teach yourself to draw the line, say no, and refrain from committing to things you can't follow through with.

Stand Out as a Role Model

The best way to do this is by modeling the behavior and standards you expect from your team. Don't enforce rules that you're reluctant to keep. Some leaders make the mistake of thinking that being in leadership positions exempts them from following rules, but in reality, they have a responsibility to model these rules through their own actions. The title "leader" itself speaks volumes: It suggests that you should lead the way while others follow.

Be Responsible for Your Actions

Being a leader doesn't make you perfect. You can make mistakes and poor judgments just like everybody else. In fact, leaders are encouraged to embrace a growth mindset, and more often than not, it means trying new methods of doing things and implementing new strategies. Simply put, if you're not making mistakes, you're not trying, and chances are that you will remain stagnant or thriving in the same position with no prospects of promotion or growth. When you make mistakes, instead of blaming other people, who otherwise might not have a voice, it's best to take ownership of those mistakes and fix them. If they can't be fixed, you can learn from the experience.

Be Honest

One of the most crucial things to do in leadership is to be transparent with your team. This is not to say that you should always share every little detail concerning the organization as it depends on the situation. While some information available to you as a leader is discrete, when it comes to information that you're at liberty to share, by all means, share. People are more productive when the company is transparent because most of it directly affects their livelihood, either positively or negatively.

Be Consistent

While the above attributes make you stand out as a leader, it's consistency that will determine whether or not people will respect you.

What Makes Integrity So Crucial in Leadership?

When discussing leadership integrity, the term "ethical leadership" never fails to come up. What, then, does this term entail, and how is it integral to equity, diversity, and inclusion?

As already discussed, there's a strong correlation between leadership integrity and trust when it comes to leader-employee relations. Of interest to mention is the dynamic that surrounds it: While leaders tend to be judged on their character and competence, employees tend to associate leadership integrity with kindness. They view leaders with integrity as those with genuine intentions for them and the organization rather than selfish motives (Klaussen, 2020).

Moreover, some people consider entrepreneurial leadership an umbrella term that sums up all the best leadership traits. It is characterized by traits such as the ability to navigate uncertainty, manage risk, and explore ambiguity. Some believe a combination of these qualities produces the most effective results in leadership. This can be attributed to the ability of successful entrepreneurial leaders to adapt, change, and innovate in times of crisis.

However, despite the importance of these traits, the question of why integrity is crucial in leadership remains unanswered. To address this inquiry, let's examine how integrity manifests in leadership across various contexts (Klaussen, 2020):

Conscious Leadership

According to Raj Sisodia, a professor at Babson College, conscious leadership can benefit not only individuals and companies but also society as a whole while boosting profits. Sisodia, who teaches marketing at Babson, is the founder and driving force behind the Conscious Capitalism movement, which is inspired by his book of the same name.

Raj Sisodia's latest book, *The Healing Organization*, envisions a world where organizations prioritize the best interests of their customers by upholding values such as fairness, truth, beauty, and basic goodness (Sisodia, 2019). In fact, should they have any queries, they are encouraged to stand up for these principles. In this ideal world, companies have passionate and loyal employees who love coming to work. Additionally, because they contribute positively to their communities and preserve the ecosystem they operate in, they do not struggle with customer or employee retention.

If envisioning this makes you wish you had this kind of impact in your leadership role, know that this is achievable. You only need to have integrity because without it, there's no honesty, kindness, and, most importantly, trust. People are drawn to people they can trust, and this remains true in a business setup. The results of integrity in conscious leadership are phenomenal and exactly what any leader would strive for: happy, motivated, and engaged employees, loyal customers, a restored ecosystem, and overall, maximum profits.

Value-Based Leadership

Babson also did exceptionally good work around value-based leadership, and its commitment is portrayed by the amazing work of Mary C. Gentile, a senior fellow in social innovation and the author of *Giving Voice to Values: How to Speak Your Mind When You Know What's Right*. Gentile seeks to answer the question of what ethical leadership entails and why it is crucial.

According to Gentile, *Giving Voice to Values* can be considered an innovative approach to understanding, discussing, and teaching how to act on our values in the workplace (Klaussen, 2020). This values-driven leadership approach acknowledges that leaders simply need to make their teams aware of their values. However, it does not stop there; there should be preparation for effective values-based action.

These preparations require dedication from leaders. They need to create and set in place scripts and plans to address common justifications for questionable practices. Needless to say, having integrity as a leader is critical to handling these conflicts.

Diversity, Equity, and Inclusion Committee

Diversity, equity, and inclusion (DEI) are integral components of leadership integrity because they reflect a leader's commitment to treating all individuals with respect and fairness. Leaders need to start recognizing the importance of creating an inclusive environment where their employees can feel valued, seen, and appreciated for the work they do and the value they add to the organization rather than their race, ethnicity, gender, and more. However, this is only achievable if leaders are willing to lead with empathy and encourage a culture of open communication. They should also be willing to actively work to address and eliminate discrimination and bias. By prioritizing DEI, leaders demonstrate their commitment to ethical and moral principles, which are fundamental to leadership integrity.

Babson faculty members are currently taking action to drive change in response to the social injustices that have been observed in our society. As an initial step, they have established a new Committee on Diversity, Equity, and Inclusion. Babson recognizes that saying the right things without taking any action does not yield any positive results in business. Consequently, the committee aims to incorporate diversity, equity, and inclusion into the fundamental aspects of the faculty, planning, and curriculum through strategic efforts. This highlights the importance of leadership integrity, where doing the right thing is essential.

Finally, leaders must prioritize integrity in their actions and decisions to promote diversity and inclusivity. It is up to each and every one of us to create a culture that values and celebrates differences. Let us challenge ourselves to reflect on our biases, educate ourselves on the experiences of marginalized communities, and take intentional steps toward creating a more equitable and inclusive world. Therefore, I challenge and encourage all leaders to join me in committing to lead with integrity and champion diversity and inclusivity in all aspects of our lives.

The Leader With Integrity

The leader with integrity consistently demonstrates honesty, transparency, and ethical behavior in all of their actions and decision-making processes. Moreover, this leader prioritizes the greater good of their organization, community, or society over their personal gain or interests. The importance of integrity in leadership cannot be overstated, as it inspires trust, respect, and loyalty among employees and creates a positive organizational culture.

Chapter 2

Effective Leadership Calls for Strong Communication Skills

*T*he more we learn about effective communication, the better we'll be at leading, as our directives will be better understood. – Paul Jarvis

As a leader, you should be able to clearly convey information, instructions, ideas, or feedback to your teams, stakeholders, and subordinates without bias and in a way that does not belittle or offend the next person. This chapter will encourage you to enhance your communication skills by teaching you what strong communication entails and how it benefits the organization.

Why Effective Leadership Begins with Communication

When it comes to effective leadership, communication goes beyond conveying information: You should be able to connect with your team in a way that encourages and motivates them to work. If the way you communicate does not create alignment throughout the team or organization, it's time to reevaluate your communication skills. Communication is a very crucial part of effective leadership because, without it, the organization can be in total chaos. Notably, although 75% of employees recognize effective communication as the most important leadership attribute, only 33% believe their leaders communicate effectively (Jouany & Martic, 2023).

While some people were born with the ability to communicate effectively, others have to acquire this skill, and if you're one of them, that's totally okay. Communication skills can be taught and enhanced; you just have to be consistent with your efforts. As a leader, you should be able to communicate effectively on a one-on-one level, in relatively small groups, and with a big audience. You should even be able to communicate well when you're under pressure or when you're put on the spot. While this sounds complicated, it can be done.

Let's take a look at some of the reasons why effective communication is so vital in leadership (Why Effective Leadership Starts With Communication, n.d.):

Creating Alignment

It's important for employees to align with the organization's vision, strategy, and goals at an individual and team level. If people don't know what they are working towards, how can they be expected to produce appropriate results? It is the duty of leaders to effectively relay or articulate the company vision or goals to their teams and ensure that the strategy to realize these goals is well-communicated and understood. Moreover, leaders need to communicate this information to their teams in a way that resonates with them to generate buy-in. In addition to effective verbal or written communication, it's also crucial for leaders to communicate by way of action. If the vision is important, they should show it by how much discipline, drive, and hard work they themselves are willing to put into it. This way, their teams can follow their lead and prioritize the same vision. The truth is that with leadership comes a great responsibility to lead by example, and if you don't take a project seriously, chances are that your team will follow in your footsteps.

Inspiring Connection and Inspiration

Leaders have a duty to inspire their teams, especially in times of change and crisis. If you speak with doubt, uncertainty, and fear, then chances are your team will be demotivated. However, when you speak with confidence, boldness, and optimism, people will not only understand your message without fear clouding their judgment, but they will also be inspired. Business has to continue whether or not there's doubt or crisis surrounding it, and effective leaders are able to communicate in a way that ensures, reassures, and inspires, even when in doubt.

Take, for example, the COVID-19 pandemic. Effective communication came in handy to the success of change management and for businesses to continue their operations smoothly. Companies had to adopt remote work arrangements, which required clear communication of new policies and procedures, such as virtual meeting protocols, communication tools, and work schedules. In addition, companies had to ensure that employees had access to the necessary resources and support, such as technology, equipment, and training, to work effectively from home.

Furthermore, businesses had to communicate effectively with their customers and suppliers to manage the impact of the pandemic on their operations. This included communicating changes in delivery times, stock availability, and safety measures to ensure the health and well-being of customers and employees. Most importantly, effective communication helped businesses to maintain employee morale and engagement during that difficult and uncertain period.

It goes without saying that leaders who communicated regularly and transparently with their employees about the challenges and opportunities of the pandemic were more likely to retain their staff and maintain their productivity and motivation.

Finally, when it comes to inspiring connection and inspiration, active listening also comes into play. Building a connection with your team and being in a position to inspire them to be productive regardless of the situation requires you to listen.

Therefore, solicit feedback, pay attention to their body language, and create time to listen to their grievances. People need to know that their feelings are valid and their voices matter. You're in a better position to give reassurance and guide your teams accordingly when you know their perspective on issues.

Implementing Strategy

While leaders are in a position to create strategies, they should be able to implement these techniques successfully. This is not to say that there's no room for mistakes, as a growth mindset requires it, but it's one thing to devise a strategy on paper, and it's another to put it into action. You should know how to effectively communicate strategies to employees so that they fully know what is expected of them, how to deliver, and when. Leaders at any level should have the skill to communicate strategies effectively to their teams. Additionally, it's equally important to create two-way communication channels when executing strategies because teams can suggest better or more efficient ways of doing things, share ideas, and overall provide feedback at every stage of the project.

Strategies for Achieving Effective Leadership Communication

You can't separate effective communication from effective leadership—the two work hand in hand. When communication is done properly, leaders inspire trust and productivity. However, their silence or lack of clear communication speaks volumes, and it can negatively affect the organization. How, then, can leaders communicate in a way that promotes productivity and trust and gives the organization a sustainable competitive advantage? Let's get right into it (Leading Effectively Staff, 2023):

Be Simple and Direct

Be direct when you communicate, and always say exactly what you mean. Avoid flowery language and indirect talk; people are not going to read your mind. A lot of communication is done virtually now, and being direct helps to keep the listeners engaged and interested.

Make Your Expectations Clear

Make it a point to establish clear expectations and norms for your team. After doing this, ensure that your own words and actions align with the norms you create for others. You have to lead by example at all times.

Know Your People

Knowing your people will help you to influence and lead them accordingly. People are different, and what works for one may not work for another. This means that you have to tailor your message or strategy to suit the audience. For example, an emotional person may be easily swayed by an emotional approach compared to a logical one and vice versa. Moreso, an extrovert might be more excited about work trips and social events than an introvert.

Be Relentless

Workplace communication is an ongoing process. Therefore, leave all methods of communication open and create an atmosphere where your team is comfortable giving you feedback and communicating their grievances or fears to you. Avoid being arrogant and find time to converse with your team members individually. The more you know them, the easier it is to inspire productivity. Try to be as transparent as possible.

Be Prepared

Some levels of communication require preparation beforehand. If you're going to address people during a meeting or conference, then go through the trouble of being adequately prepared. Whether you prepare a PowerPoint presentation or jot down your minutes using pen and paper, make sure your delivery is organized, easy to understand, and to the point.

Be Open to Receiving Feedback

People appreciate it when their voices are heard and when their opinions are valued. Asking for feedback is a tactic that will help you gain the trust and respect of your team. However, don't just use this as a method to gain respect, but make an effort to genuinely value your team's feedback. Don't just take it into consideration; put it into action if it's worthy. Leaders do not know it all, and they are not always right, and when they give their teams a voice, they create powerful collaborations. Taking your team's feedback seriously will also help you grow by enhancing your leadership skills. However, while taking your team's feedback seriously will help to build trust, ignoring it will do the opposite. Failure to follow feedback with actions will lead people to think that you don't take them seriously or that their opinions are invalid, which may cause resentment.

Don't Be Afraid to Initiate Tough but Necessary Conversations

Conflict resolution skills are part of leadership, and rather than ignoring conflict to keep the peace, try to tackle difficult conversations for the greater good. Workplace conflict is inevitable, and how it's handled will determine whether or not involved parties will continue working together in harmony. Moreover, as a leader, you will find yourself being the mediator, and one of the best ways to do this is being neutral, listening to each side of the story, and avoiding bias in your verdict and way forward. Do whatever you can to encourage open communication as a way to resolve conflict.

Ask Questions

The most effective way to encourage two-way communication is by asking questions. Effective communication is not merely just talking and making your opinions or strategies known; it's about making time to listen to your audience. It's in doing so that you will learn whether or not they understood or accepted your message.

Additionally, leaders who are humble enough to listen to their teams can easily earn their respect, support, and trust.

Read the Room

You can learn a lot about your audience by studying their non-verbal cues. Whether they are agreeable, engaged, confused, understanding, or even bored, you can always pick it up if you pay attention and adjust your message accordingly to get their full engagement and total support. When people understand your message and are aligned with it, they often indicate this by nodding their heads, asking questions, and making eye contact. However, when they are not aligned, you will often see your audience leaning back with their arms crossed or portraying confused and bored expressions on their faces. Moreover, it's always smart to ask questions as a way to keep your audience hooked and give them a voice.

Use Stories to Illustrate

Sharing a compelling story breathes life into a vision, goal, or objective. Such narratives instill trust, captivate hearts and minds, and serve as a constant reminder of the vision. Stories are easier to recite and recall compared to mission statements, project plans, or strategy documents, making them crucial in communicating the vision. Developing and articulating an authentic, daring, and compelling story can strengthen your leadership brand. Also, if you've ever caught sight of your staff members yawning throughout a meeting, you know how discouraging or frustrating that can be. The good news is that using stories to illustrate your points can make things easier to understand and much less tedious.

Use Body Language to Reinforce Intent

Demonstrating positive body language, such as maintaining eye contact, nodding in agreement, and using relaxed gestures, can motivate your team members and put them at ease when communicating with you. Even a simple nod or smile can go a long way in showing that you're attentive and empathetic, and over time, these small gestures can add up to establish deeper connections and enhance collaboration. For instance, when a team member shares their innovative idea during a brainstorming session, maintaining eye contact and nodding in approval can encourage them to continue contributing to the conversation. By consistently incorporating positive body language, you can create a more inclusive and supportive organizational culture where everyone feels valued and respected.

Listen Attentively and Encourage Staff Input

Failing to listen to your team members can have serious consequences. When employees are not heard, they may feel undervalued, unappreciated, and disengaged from their work. In some cases, they may even become resentful or seek employment elsewhere. In order to prevent this, it's essential to seek out and actively listen to individuals from all levels of the organization, including key stakeholders with differing opinions and new employees who may be hesitant to speak up. By demonstrating empathy and creating psychological safety, you can help team members feel valued and comfortable sharing their ideas and concerns. This, in turn, shows that you care about both your employees and the organization as a whole.

Furthermore, it's important to be comfortable with silence and encourage others to offer their ideas and solutions before sharing your own. By listening 80% of the time and talking only 20% of the time, you demonstrate respect and interest in your colleagues, which can build trust and establish emotional connections crucial for effective leadership. By implementing these strategies, you can foster a more collaborative and inclusive work environment where all team members feel heard and valued.

Affirm with Your Actions

Effective leaders understand that communication goes beyond words. While mastering clear and compelling language is important, leaders must also align their behavior with their words to maintain credibility and build trust with their team. If there's a disconnect between what a leader says and how they act, their credibility can be undermined. Therefore, it's crucial to focus on alignment and be intentional about the messages conveyed through behavior and actions, even when no words are spoken. A leader who demands punctuality from their team, for example, must also be punctual to demonstrate the importance of this value. Similarly, a leader who advocates for work-life balance must make sure to practice it themselves. By leading by example, leaders can communicate their values and priorities in a more powerful and authentic way, creating a more trusting and respectful work environment.

Involve Your Team Before Deciding or Concluding on a Plan of Action

Effective communication is a critical component of successful leadership, but it's only the first step in achieving organizational goals. After the exchange, it's essential to take what has been learned and synthesize it into a coherent plan that can be presented to the appropriate stakeholders. This plan should reflect the ideas and concerns of all parties involved and should be crafted with the goal of generating buy-in and ensuring that everyone is on the same page before executing a strategy.

The process of generating buy-in involves more than simply persuading others to support your plan. It requires creating a shared vision that aligns with the values and priorities of all stakeholders, including employees, customers, shareholders, and partners. By involving all parties in the planning process, leaders can create a sense of ownership and commitment that can lead to greater engagement, motivation, and loyalty.

The success of any strategy depends on the ability to achieve buy-in and alignment across the organization. By taking the time to listen, synthesize, and present a clear and compelling plan, leaders can ensure that everyone is working towards the same goal, reducing friction and increasing the likelihood of success.

Keep Your Reputation in Mind

As a leader, your reputation is one of your most valuable assets. It can take years to build a positive reputation, but it takes only a few missteps to damage it irreparably. Therefore, it's crucial to always prioritize your reputation over the immediate needs of communication. While effective communication is vital for achieving your goals and building relationships with your team, you must never compromise your reputation for the sake of communication.

As you navigate the challenges of leadership communication, it's essential to find the right balance between being too aggressive and being too relaxed. If you lean too heavily in one direction, you risk getting a reputation that can damage your leadership image and undermine your ability to lead effectively. To avoid this, consider asking yourself thought-provoking questions that can help you clarify your communication style, such as "When should I stay out of an issue?", "When should I get involved?", or "What's the appropriate response for when errors are identified?"

Additionally, it can be helpful to solicit feedback from colleagues or mentors to gain a better understanding of how your communication style is perceived. Make a list of communication concerns you have, and ask a trusted colleague to describe the behaviors they would consider either too aggressive or too relaxed. Their responses can provide valuable insight into adjusting your communication style to better align with your goals and values while maintaining your reputation. By prioritizing your reputation and seeking feedback, you can ensure that your communication style is consistent with your leadership brand and build trust and respect among your team.

Inadequate Communication in a Professional Environment

Every organization running smoothly and successfully has established the importance of effective communication at a leadership level. While most people think of effective communication as the ability to successfully hold verbal interactions, it goes beyond that. Written communication, body language, tone of voice, and other forms of non-verbal communication all come into play. The importance of workplace communication is far-reaching, and when it's done poorly, the consequences are serious for both individuals and the organization as a whole. Workplace communication affects everything from productivity and efficiency to employee satisfaction and retention.

Role ambiguity is prominent in organizations with poor communication skills. Employees are constantly confused about their roles and responsibilities, and as a result, they may start missing deadlines. In general, productivity is negatively affected in this situation. Moreover, where role ambiguity is prominent, misunderstandings and conflict may also arise. As a result, employee morale may decrease, leading to increased absenteeism and turnover. Overall, there will be a lack of trust between leaders and their teams, which hinders collaboration and innovation.

Additionally, businesses with a poor communication culture may fail to communicate adequately with customers and clients. Consequently, these business clients get a bad reputation and even face legal issues. Therefore, it's crucial for leaders to foster a culture of effective communication and maintain it in all aspects of their daily business operations.

This section explores the different consequences of poor communication in the workplace and highlights the importance of clear and concise communication in achieving organizational success.

Consequences of Poor Communication in the Workplace

During my early experience as a leader, I neglected to give proper guidance to a new engineer on how to carry out a small construction project in compliance with the company's safety protocols. Due to my inadequate guidance and failure to provide clear and specific instructions, the inexperienced engineer was left confused and made errors while attempting to carry out a small construction project in compliance with the company's safety policies. As a result, the construction team did not fully adhere to the safety protocols, leading to a near-miss incident involving dropped equipment. Additionally, I neglected to provide a timeline for the task, causing the engineer to use the wrong resources and take longer than expected to complete the project. This lack of clear guidance also caused the engineer to feel overwhelmed and unmotivated, resulting in decreased productivity and insufficient preparation time for the task.

This scenario emphasizes the significance of providing clear and concise instructions in the workplace. Ambiguity in instructions can result in misunderstandings and miscommunications, which can negatively affect the organization's progress and even pose a threat to employee safety. Therefore, it is crucial to provide employees with explicit instructions and expectations to ensure that tasks are performed accurately, safely, and efficiently. Moreover, it helps employees develop confidence in their skills and motivates them to accomplish their tasks clearly. Effective communication, characterized by clarity and conciseness, is a pivotal factor that plays a crucial role in achieving organizational success.

Effective communication should be a mutual process in the workplace. While it is essential to provide employees with clear instructions, it is equally vital to encourage them to seek clarification and provide feedback. This approach helps to ensure that tasks are accomplished accurately and that employees understand their roles and responsibilities. As a manager, I realized the importance of giving timely progress updates and providing constructive feedback to help employees enhance their skills and stay on course. I also recognized that providing employees with the right tools, resources, and support is crucial to achieving organizational success. In essence, creating an environment where employees feel free to ask questions, give feedback, and have access to the necessary resources is a key factor in promoting open communication, enhancing productivity, and achieving organizational goals.

To sum up, effective communication is crucial for organizational success. My failure to provide clear instructions in a safety-sensitive area could have led to a severe incident, highlighting the importance of clear communication, especially in such areas. Misunderstandings and miscommunications caused by unclear instructions can hinder the organization's progress. Providing employees with adequate information and allowing them to seek clarification and feedback ensures that tasks are completed accurately and efficiently. I was able to learn from this experience, and one of the first things I emphasize to young and upcoming leaders is the importance of offering timely updates and constructive feedback. When leaders do this, they create room for employees to stay focused and develop their skills. Overall, by promoting clear and concise communication in the workplace, organizations can foster an environment of collaboration and productivity, enabling their teams to work together effectively and achieve success.

Examples of Effective Communication in the Workplace

Clear communication can give any workplace the order and efficiency needed to function well. Let's take a look at how clear communication remedied a role ambiguity situation and aided with change management in these two cases.

Effective Communication and Role Ambiguity

John was a new hire at a tech company, and he was excited to start his new role. However, he quickly realized that there was some confusion around his job responsibilities. His job description was somewhat vague, and he wasn't sure which projects he was supposed to work on and to whom he was supposed to report.

At first, John tried to figure things out on his own. He spent a lot of time reading company documents and talking to his colleagues, but he still couldn't get a clear understanding of his role.

Finally, John decided to schedule a meeting with his manager, Sarah. He explained his concerns and asked her to clarify his job responsibilities. Sarah was receptive and explained that the company was going through a transition period, which had caused some role ambiguity. She apologized for the confusion and assured John that they would work together to resolve the issue.

Over the next few days, Sarah and John had several conversations to clarify John's role. Sarah also introduced him to other team members and made sure he understood their roles and responsibilities. She provided him with detailed feedback on his work and answered any questions he had.

Through effective communication, John was able to gain clarity on his job responsibilities and feel more confident in his role. He was able to contribute to the team's projects and work effectively with his colleagues. The experience taught John the importance of clear communication in the workplace and helped him build a strong working relationship with his manager.

Effective Communication and Change Management

Managing change in the workplace can be challenging, but effective communication is a crucial tool for helping employees adapt and navigate through change. One example of this was when many companies underwent a significant restructuring process during the COVID-19 pandemic.

Most restructuring processes involved changes to reporting structures, policies and procedures, and job responsibilities, which caused many employees to feel worried about the impact of these changes on their careers. Some employees were even resistant to the changes. During this period, leaders who recognized the importance of effective communication developed a comprehensive communication plan that included regular updates and online meetings to make up for in-person meetings with employees.

During these online meetings, most went to great lengths to explain how the restructuring and changes would affect employees. They also provided opportunities for employees to ask questions and voice their concerns. As a result, these meetings allowed employees to discuss their specific roles and responsibilities according to the new order and receive feedback on their performance.

Moreover, leaders also provided ongoing communication throughout the process, with regular updates through emails, company intranet, and follow-up meetings to ensure that everyone was at ease, felt involved in decision-making, and had the information they needed to carry out their jobs effectively.

Through effective communication, many companies were able to successfully manage the much-needed change process. Employees felt informed and supported and were able to navigate through the changes with ease. Some even embraced the changes and saw new opportunities for growth and development within their organizations.

This experience highlights the importance of open and transparent communication during times of change. By being proactive and keeping employees informed, leaders can build trust and ensure a smooth transition for everyone involved.

Communicating Company Changes

There have been many times I have had to communicate with my teams on changes or events that were affecting the company. However, those communications do not always feel personable or address all the concerns. As a leader, I've had to tell my teams about changes or events that were happening in the company. But sometimes, the way I communicated didn't feel very personal and didn't address all their concerns. To make sure I cover everything that's important to my team, I get talking points from our communication groups.

Take an event where the company I was working through had a huge significant restructuring event that affected nearly every level. There was widespread worry about office closures, downsizing, or changes; even I didn't know if my job was at risk. I had to provide the confidence that was expected by the corporate communication directive, explaining the information that was available to be shared.

I reframed the information into four sections: the introduction, the company goals, the framework, and the conclusion. I made each section relevant and personal to my team because no two teams are the same. Here is an example of what I did to communicate such an impactful message.

Communication Introduction

Organizational structure is an important component of any company as it dictates the way in which tasks are done, how decisions are made, and how employees are managed. When an organization makes a significant change to its structure, it can have a lasting impact on its employees. I know this message will impact each of you, and your concerns and worries are different. Let me explain what I know about how this significant organizational structure change will affect you and your fellow employees, and we can discuss some strategies for mitigating any negative impacts that you or your fellow employees may feel.

Identifying Your Company's Goals

I always spend time on *why* we are doing this. In this example, when an organization makes a significant change to its structure, it is important to identify the goals of the change. What is the purpose of the change? What are the expected outcomes? How will the change affect employees? Answering these questions can help managers understand the impact of the change and plan for any necessary adjustments. In our particular situation, we were trying to streamline and improve support across the company, reduce the cost structure, and help build bridges across our various assets.

Crafting the Communication Framework

As it was clearly outlined in corporate communications, effective communication is key when making significant changes to an organization's structure. Employees need to be informed of the changes and understand their implications. Managers should create a communication framework with a timeline for communicating the changes and a strategy for engaging with employees. Managers should also consider how they will address questions and concerns and ensure that all employees are informed of the changes.

In this particular instance, our company had some employee assist avenues, but I am unsure if my team really reached out to those. For my strategy, I used the general announcement in a team meeting then followed up with each one separately. In my one-on-one meetings, I asked endless open-ended questions to get a sense of how my team was doing with the stress of the change. I was using a rule of only talking about 20% of the time.

Some individuals were very open, some were still processing, and some did not really want to speak. Regardless of how open they were, I continued to follow up with each member at least weekly, and some needed more support.

Implementation

At some point, a leader will be asked to act on implementing changes. Once the communication framework is in place, managers should begin the process of implementing the changes. For larger actions driven by the company, this may be dictated to you, but for smaller changes on the team, you will have the power to implement them quickly. This may involve employee training, changes to job roles and responsibilities, or even the introduction of new technology. Managers should ensure that employees are aware of and equipped to handle the changes. Employees should also be provided with support and resources to help them adjust to the new structure. Keep using your framework that was developed through this change of implementation.

Communication Conclusion

There will be a conclusion to making these changes that will come in the form of acceptance. In my example of making a significant change to an organization's structure, it will have a major impact on employees. Some employees who have the largest impact, like demotions or location change, may take a year or so before they feel like they fit back into a team. Managers need to identify the goals of the change and create a communication framework to inform employees of the changes. Team leaders should also implement the changes effectively, providing employees with training, resources, and support to ensure a smooth transition. By following these steps, managers can help mitigate any negative impacts of a significant organizational structure change. Lastly, just listen to each member with empathy. You may not be able to change their situation, but you can be a confident leader who listens and finds little ways to help them accept the change. This can only be done through effective communication.

The Leader Who Communicates Effectively

An effective leader should possess excellent communication skills, including active listening, clarity in conveying ideas, empathy towards their audience, and the ability to tailor their communication style to suit their audience. They should be approachable, transparent, and open to feedback while also being able to provide constructive feedback themselves. Additionally, a good leader should foster a culture of open communication within their team and encourage their team members to share their ideas and opinions. Effective communication is essential for building trust, fostering collaboration, and achieving shared goals.

Chapter 3

Leadership Vision— Cultivating Your Leadership Capabilities

A leader has the vision and conviction that a dream can be achieved. He inspires the power and energy to get it done. – Ralph Lauren

Can you really call yourself a leader if you don't have a vision? This is not to discourage but to point out a very vital role that can never be separated from leadership. If you're a leader without a vision in place, where are you leading your team? To fully develop your leadership capabilities, you need to have a vision. It allows you to imagine a future that is different from the present and inspires others to work towards it. A clear leadership vision provides direction, purpose, and motivation for individuals and teams to achieve their goals.

A Leader's Vision

In order to be a highly respected leader, you need to gain your team's support. Although that may sound complicated because people can be difficult to please, one simple and effective way to do this is to set clear goals and communicate them to your team so that they all understand them. Everyone is an adult at work; they prefer to be roped in because every decision made for the company affects them. You might have the power to make decisions and set goals, but you need people's buy-in and support for those goals to be realized. It's unwise to have a vision and not make an effort to sit your staff down and break it down to them because people hardly appreciate being caught unaware and told to change the course of their actions or adopt new rules altogether.

You might be wondering what exactly leadership vision entails. A vision is simply defined as a clear, specific, and distinctive view of the future, which is usually connected to strategic advances aligned with the organization. What separates effective leadership from ineffective leadership is not necessarily the lack of a vision but the inability or reluctance to communicate it in a way that fosters enthusiasm, drive, and commitment from your team. You have to be able to inspire others to work towards a certain goal; otherwise, you're just a manager and hardly a leader.

Of interest to mention is how your vision as a leader can build trust. This is because your vision and the strategies you implement to realize that vision reflect your views on the organization in terms of what it can be rather than what it is. What builds and solidifies trust lies not only in your ability to communicate your vision but your consistency and willingness to demonstrate how to make that vision a reality. Leaders shouldn't just yell orders, but they should be able to get their hands dirty from time to time.

Leadership vision is essential, and it contributes to the organization's overall success. This kind of vision should not only be understood through every function of the organization but indicative of the direction in which the company is headed towards. The more this vision is understood and supported by staff, the more effective it is in directing their daily functions, activities, and behaviors.

Although some people use the words vision and mission interchangeably, they have distinctively different meanings. While an organization's mission defines a purpose, vision refers to its direction. In other words, the mission provides a framework for decision-making, and your vision should align with it.

Finally, in today's competitive business world, you need to have a vision that's based on a forecast of business events. You should aim to keep the business competitive in the face of business rivalries, new entries, and imitations. You should also have a plan in place for when unforeseen changes happen. The COVID-19 pandemic taught everyone how unpredictable life is, and many organizations suffered—some have not been able to function effectively until today. In my opinion, this separated the leaders from the managers, and companies with solid visions, leaders who are critical thinkers, and congruent teams were able to stand through it all.

Practical Steps to Develop and Hone Your Visionary Communication Skills

Everything takes practice, and if you have not been effectively communicating your vision, you're not less of a leader—you just need to practice. You're in that position because you not only earned it but you showed great potential to usher the organization forward. Here's a detailed and yet simple practice you can use to develop your visionary communication skills (Zmorenski, n.d.):

Step 1: Consider a challenge your organization, department, or division has been facing.

Step 2: Imagine or visualize the big picture. If the situation were to be effectively improved, how incredible would your success be as a result? How will this newfound success benefit employees and the organization as a whole? No dream is too big, and not even the sky's the limit in this situation. Be a visionary, and don't limit your mind.

Step 3: Try to figure out how you will effectively communicate your vision. In what setting will you communicate this vision, and what sort of words and phrases are you going to use? Are you going to communicate the vision to the managers or supervisors first? Is it going to be during a staff meeting or during a one-on-one session? And finally, how are you going to communicate the benefits associated with this vision? It's wise to write down your ideas at this point.

Step 4: At this stage, you can practice communicating all the things you have written down. Say it out loud to either yourself or others and see if it's believable. Make sure your communication is clear, concise, and sincere, and remember, if you don't believe in your own vision, other people won't.

Once you're done with these steps and ready to communicate your vision, remember to use it to inspire and motivate your team and not to dictate. It is your team's buy-in that will help make this vision a reality. Communicate how it will benefit them and the organization and how the vision will help the business to sustain a competitive advantage so that everyone can continue benefiting from their jobs. Letting your team decide the steps to take towards achieving this goal will motivate them even further as they will feel included. You should be able to give your team a vision, then step away and give them room to devise strategies that work for them to achieve it. That is part of what makes a great leader: giving people the autonomy they need to stay motivated.

Creating Your Leadership Vision

Think of any wealthy or famous person; you will realize that you don't know them for the way they managed minutes on a daily basis or how they randomly rose to the occasion when their organizations faced a challenge. No, the likes of Steve Jobs and Bill Gates are known because their strong leadership vision propelled them to the highest levels of success.

You might have learned the importance of creating a mission and vision statement for the organization when you were in college, but now that you're on the job, leadership vision continues to be the most sought-after among others. Have you ever asked yourself why? The answer is simple: Leaders do not have a vision—they are their vision. Vision affects every little decision they make on a daily basis. Below are some of the most effective ways to create a leadership vision (How to Build Your Leadership Vision, n.d):

Self-Reflection

Self-awareness goes a long way in determining why you do what you do. Why did you choose your career path and what motivates you to wake up each day with the drive to keep things moving? These types of questions will help you get in touch with your inner self in a way that allows you to determine your vision. Self-awareness isn't an overnight thing, so don't feel discouraged if you can't get in touch with your inner self instantly—it takes time. But once you do, you will develop belief and certainty in yourself in a way that's unshakeable.

Mindfulness

Having a leadership position can sometimes get so overwhelming that you forget to slow down and unwind. However, if you want to deepen your self-reflection in a way that allows you to gain new insights and contribute significantly to your leadership vision, try practicing mindfulness. To achieve this, you can practice meditation, yoga, or priming. These activities are not a waste of time that you would have otherwise utilized to be productive in your role. On the contrary, they promote productivity, reduce stress, and help you stay focused. Great leaders use unrivaled focus to create a vision and stay aligned with the outcomes.

Positivity

One of the most underrated character traits a leader should have is optimism. In the face of challenges, change, and uncertainty, you have to be able to keep your head above water and speak to your people in a way that gives them hope. Similarly, no one wants to work on a vision that is focused on problems and characterized by endless challenges. You need to look beyond challenges and offer solutions, keep your people motivated against all odds, and help maintain their job security in spite of the internal or external situation of the business. That is effective leadership. A key aspect of leadership vision is the ability to identify problems, empower individuals to create solutions, and have faith in your team's ability to work collaboratively towards implementing those solutions.

Clarity

There's no real difference between a dark and unclear future. It's important to ensure that your vision is clear. Utilize PowerPoint presentations and anything that plainly outlines the step-by-step process of your vision. Be ready to answer the big questions like why, how, and when in a clear and concise manner. Communicating your vision takes patience; not everyone is going to show enthusiasm, and not everyone is going to understand your vision the moment you say it out loud. Therefore, you need to be ready to explain each stage of your vision and how it benefits the organization. Refrain from making commands or getting angry when people don't understand the vision from the onset. The secret is to make it as clear as possible and give people the level of autonomy that gives them fulfillment. People need to feel like they are waking up to make a difference in the world, and ensuring that your vision gives them that will motivate them to wake up each day to show up and do their best to realize it.

Communication

Being able to communicate your vision effectively is as crucial as the vision itself. Once you're sure that you have a clear and concise vision that will offer solutions to problems and usher the organization forward, communicate your vision with your team; you should never assume that they will just know what it is if you don't tell them. Even when you tell them the vision, follow up:

- You *can* ask questions to make sure that they understand the fundamental points.

- You *can* write your vision statement down

and send it to every individual whose contribution is needed to make it a reality. That way, they will always refer to it when they are confused.

- You *can* set milestones for your vision is a wise way to measure success along the way.

Don't forget to announce success and relate it to the vision so that your team stays encouraged. Moreover, when you give feedback, make sure you commend everyone for their hard work and point out specifics of what they are doing right and how much you appreciate it. When it comes to criticism, make sure it's constructive and phrased in a way that doesn't discourage your team.

Action

Nothing gives your team confidence in your vision more than your belief in it. To show that you believe in your vision, you need to act towards achieving it. Although you have the power to cascade it down and delegate, when you go the extra mile to be hands-on with your project, you give your team the confidence to do the same. Many things you will do as a leader will require you to lead by example through your actions as much as your words. When your vision is strong and you believe in it, you will not hesitate to make tough decisions and achieve challenging goals, and you will take determined action for each milestone from start to finish.

The Leader With Vision

One example I experienced around leadership vision is when I was working as an engineering manager in field operations. There was a need to update the company's technology controls of multiple facilities, but the budget did not allow for an expensive overhaul. I had a previous leader who would always say, "When you cannot eat the whole apple, find a way to take bites of the apple until you finish it." I had the vision to move forward with a less expensive solution that could be implemented gradually over several years. This solution was to break the solution into multiple components and multiple systems, allowing us to invest in the necessary technology while still maintaining a reasonable budget each year.

The company was able to successfully implement new technology without significant upfront costs due to this vision. We also achieved cost savings by completing smaller projects with internal resources. However, since the facility was several decades old, we encountered many unforeseen issues, just like when one decides to remodel a house and finds an unexpected pipe or wire. This is very common when dealing with large industrial facilities, such as when the electrical controls do not work as intended with older systems or when the wiring is in worse condition than expected.

By taking a slower approach, the engineers and operations team were able to more effectively plan for the smaller projects and address any unforeseen issues. This allowed for more thorough planning for future year budget cycles. Even though it took more time, it resulted in a successful implementation of the new technology without significant upfront costs.

The leadership vision I experienced serves as a reminder that, even when facing seemingly insurmountable odds, it is possible to succeed. By breaking down the project into smaller components and investing in the necessary technology over time, we were able to achieve the desired outcome in a cost-effective way. Additionally, the slower approach allowed us to address any unforeseen issues that arose and ultimately reach our goal. This example illustrates the importance of a clear vision and the ability to adjust when obstacles arise.

Chapter 4

Effective Leaders Are Emotionally Intelligent

No doubt emotional intelligence is rarer than book smarts, but my experience says it is actually more important in the making of a leader. You can't ignore it. – Jack Welch

Emotionally intelligent leaders are better equipped to understand their teams and, as a result, create a healthy and productive environment. This is because when people feel cared about and understood, they do their best work. What is emotional intelligence, and what makes it so crucial in leadership? This chapter will teach you all you need to know.

Emotional Intelligence Defined

Many years of leadership have taught me to identify when my staff is burned out, discouraged, or unhappy. I have also learned to react to these situations accordingly. Over the years, I have redirected people who felt lost in their roles, created more work-life balance for those who didn't know when to stop and how to say no, and motivated those who were losing enthusiasm for the vision. I'm convinced one of the most effective ways to avoid turnover and promote productivity is simply knowing your staff members and being emotionally intelligent enough to know how and when to motivate them.

What, then, is emotional intelligence? Simply put, it's the ability to recognize, understand, and regulate your emotions, as well as being able to respond to other people's emotions constructively and in a manner that creates room for better communication and empathy on a deeper level. It also allows you to identify and overcome challenges more positively.

What Is Emotional Intelligence in Leadership?

When it comes to leadership, emotional intelligence can be considered a critical skill to recognize your team's problems and offer solutions to solve them. This is why emotional intelligence is a requisite skill for each leader because, without it, teams would become chaotic and lack the coordination to function productively. If anyone wants to check a leadership style's effectiveness, they can check the level of emotional intelligence attached to it. Emotional intelligence is a term first coined by researchers John Mayer and Peter Salovey in 1990. However, with the advent of leadership roles, it has gained popularity now more than ever.

The Relevance of Emotional Intelligence in Leadership

Organizations with leaders who lack emotional intelligence can hardly survive business complexities and uncertainties. Emotional intelligence in leaders is as crucial as the skills one learns in college, and perhaps even more. Here are some of the reasons why emotional intelligence is a requisite skill for every leader (Emeritus, 2022):

- It promotes a positive work culture. When the organizational culture is positive, employees are motivated to do their jobs, leading to an increased level of productivity and efficiency.

- It encourages staff members to be innovative, which promotes creativity and growth.

- Members are constantly motivated to go the extra mile or put their best foot forward.

- It helps leaders and staff to make sound decisions and judgments in the face of challenges.

- It helps create and maintain a strong bond between a leader and their team.

Components of Emotional Intelligence in Leadership

Below are some of the most profound components of emotional intelligence in leadership (Emeritus, 2022):

Self-Awareness

When you're self-aware, you're in a position to understand your strengths and weaknesses. You also know what triggers you and what makes you happy. This helps you control your emotions and understand complex emotions that can affect your team. Self-control is a virtue for every leader because, with work pressure and people's different character traits and attitudes, it can be easy to lose your temper. But imagine what harm that would do to your reputation. In Chapter 1, I discussed leadership integrity and the importance of preserving a good reputation as a leader. Having control over your emotions is an effective way to maintain a good reputation.

Additionally, you need to be aware of your power and ability to control, lead, and guide a team. This will give you the self-confidence you need to make quick decisions, innovate, or come up with a different strategy for your organization to keep making profits and retaining its clients.

Self-Management

You need the ability to manage your emotions during challenging situations, maintain a positive outlook during uncertainty, and tackle difficult situations as they arise. Self-management will allow you to do all this and keep your head above the water during challenging business situations. It's also crucial for you to have the right reactions to challenges. Sure, you can be surprised, afraid, and uncertain, but you need to be able to promptly regain your confidence so that you can focus on finding solutions. Mental peace and a calm attitude will go a long way for you in your leadership role.

Social-Awareness

No business entity is an island as it's impossible for companies to operate in solitude. Because of this, you should always be aware of your business environment, both internally and externally. Firstly, you need to be able to understand the people you work with and manage their emotions. Likewise, it's equally important to have a deep appreciation of heterogeneous market conditions. When you do this, you can align your business strategy to the environment that surrounds it.

This is hardly possible if you don't have empathy, especially on an internal level. Without empathy, it will be difficult for you to understand people's perspectives and emotions, making it hard for your teams to communicate effectively and collaborate. In fact, according to experts, leaders with empathy are both influential and effective, owing to the fact that they have a deep appreciation of human behavior and cognition.

Relationship Management

As a leader, you will do a lot of mentoring, coaching, and conflict resolution. Relationship-management skills will help you perform these roles effectively. The more conflicts the staff has, the less satisfied they become with their jobs. You risk losing your staff to other enterprises at this point, and while some may keep showing up, they might not perform their jobs to the best of their abilities. Therefore, you need to be able to keep conflicts and miscommunication at bay to foster good productivity levels in your team.

When you understand these elements of emotional intelligence, you can be unstoppable in your role and gain respect and loyalty from your team. It's okay if you were not practicing one or more of these elements because once you start putting them into practice and seeing the rewards they can bring about, you will stand out from other leaders. Emotional intelligence is vital in every person, but this is what it looks like for a leader. Be inspired, get on board, and gain the respect and loyalty that every leader yearns for.

Traits of Emotionally Intelligent Leaders

Now that we have discussed the components of emotional intelligence, let's look at the five traits an emotionally intelligent leader would possess. This is time for some introspection; if you don't already have these traits, you can start practicing them now. It's really never too late. Let's get started:

Emotionally Intelligent Leaders are Approachable and Thoughtful

It's important for your teams to experience psychological safety through your words and actions. Are you receptive to feedback, negative or positive? Do you take responsibility for your actions or let your team take the fall for your mistakes? Do you give negative feedback in a considerate manner and show appreciation for the things your team is getting right? These are all the relevant questions you can ask yourself to determine whether or not you're creating a safe environment for your team.

Additionally, your teams should not be scared to approach you. Yes, you are the leader, but respect is not commanded by being unapproachable and creating long lines of communication such that your team members can't approach you directly. This doesn't work in your favor as it creates resentment, incongruence, and overall dissatisfaction.

Dare to be approachable, friendly, and empathetic to your team members, from the highly paid to the least. Everyone deserves respect. Lastly, be thoughtful enough to relieve someone of their duties if they are unwell or overwhelmed. Life has its challenges, and it's unrealistic to expect people to show up every day with the same enthusiasm. When you exercise this kind of thoughtfulness that shows people that their emotions, perspectives, and experiences are valued, they will put their best foot forward in their respective roles.

They Admit When They Are Wrong and Know How to Apologize

Two words: self-awareness and accountability! You should not hold yourself to a standard of perfection simply because you're a leader. Indeed, you should always double-check details before you send them or thoroughly analyze processes before you approve them, but with a busy schedule comes the very human potential to overlook something and mess them up. When you're not aware of your mistakes, you can easily blame others.

However, emotionally intelligent leaders are able to realize when they make mistakes and take accountability. When it's called for, they are not too proud to apologize. Likewise, even if you approve processes put in place by your team, if they create chaos in the workplace or cause a loss, you should take accountability for the fact that you had the final say, just the same as you would take accountability if everything went well and you were receiving praise.

Life is not simple, and neither is business. Consequently, you will make mistakes, and so will your team members. Be willing to hear them out, forgive them, and give them another chance. And when you're the one who made a mistake, be gracious and kind to yourself.

They Notice Burnout and Create Work-Life Balance

One of the things that stood out to me as a leader is how dedicated employees are willing to go the extra mile for their jobs, even at the expense of their emotional and physical well-being. They can easily miss out on family vacations, weekend events, and more to give more time to their jobs for various reasons. Some work hard so they can get promotions, some get an unhealthy addiction to their jobs, and others are afraid to lose their livelihoods. Whatever the case may be, this is not commendable, and an emotionally intelligent leader shouldn't promote this behavior.

While it's good to have dedicated and committed team members who would give their whole lives to their jobs, they can only be productive for so long. Eventually, they will get burned out, which is inevitable. With it, burnout will bring fatigue, loss of concentration, loss of interest in one's job, and more. Ultimately, productivity will decrease. As if that's not enough, you may start experiencing high absenteeism and turnover rates, poor internal relations, and decreased quality of work. You should be able to spot burnout from a distance before it causes irreversible chaos in the organization. Most importantly, you should be able to support burned-out staff and help them to observe healthy levels of work-life balance.

You might be wondering what a balanced life entails. Let's take a look at some of its aspects:

1. **Work-life balance:** Leaders should be aware of the amount of time that employees spend on work-related activities and ensure that employees have enough time for leisure and other commitments outside of work.

2. **Mental and physical health:** Leaders should be mindful of the mental and physical health of their employees and encourage them to take regular breaks throughout the day, practice self-care, and have access to mental health resources.

3. **Financial stability:** Leaders should be aware of the financial situation of their employees and ensure that they are compensated fairly and have access to services that can help them manage their finances.

Examples of Emotional Intelligence in the Workplace

The Empathetic Manager

Sarah had just been promoted to the position of manager in her company. She was excited to lead a team of five employees who were responsible for developing software applications. Sarah had always been a hard worker and had a great technical skill set, but she was also aware of the importance of emotional intelligence in the workplace.

On her first day, Sarah held a team meeting to introduce herself and get to know her team members. She noticed that one of her team members, Michael, was not very talkative and seemed uncomfortable around the others. Sarah decided to approach him after the meeting and asked if everything was okay. Michael hesitated at first, but then he opened up to Sarah and shared that he had been going through a tough time at home and was struggling to focus on work. Sarah listened attentively and showed empathy toward Michael's situation.

Over the next few days, Sarah made a point of checking in on Michael and offering him support whenever he needed it. She also gave him more flexible deadlines to help him manage his workload better. As a result, Michael started to open up more and feel more comfortable around the team. He became more engaged in his work, and his productivity improved.

One day, Sarah noticed that another team member, Alex, was becoming increasingly stressed and anxious. Sarah could see that Alex was working long hours and seemed overwhelmed by the workload. Instead of ignoring the issue, Sarah decided to take a proactive approach. She arranged a one-on-one meeting with Alex to discuss his workload and offered to help him prioritize his tasks. She also suggested that they could look at ways to delegate some of the work to other team members. Alex was grateful for Sarah's support and felt more motivated to tackle his work.

Sarah's empathy and active listening skills continued to be an asset to her team. She made an effort to get to know each team member on a personal level and showed interest in their lives outside of work. Encouraging open communication provided a safe space for her team to express their concerns or ideas.

One day, Sarah received feedback from her team members during a performance review. They shared that they felt supported by her leadership style and appreciated her ability to understand and respond to their individual needs. Sarah was thrilled to hear this and knew that building strong relationships with her team was key to their success.

As time passed, Sarah's team became more productive, and their projects started to receive positive recognition from the company's leadership. Sarah was proud of her team's achievements, but more importantly, she was proud of the relationships that she had built with her team members. She knew that emotional intelligence was a critical factor in building a positive workplace culture, and she was committed to continuing to develop her own emotional intelligence skills.

In conclusion, Sarah's story demonstrates how emotional intelligence can significantly impact a team's performance and well-being. By showing empathy, active listening, and proactive problem-solving skills, Sarah was able to build trust with her team members and create a positive work environment. Her story is a reminder that leadership goes beyond technical skills and that emotional intelligence is an essential aspect of effective leadership.

Chapter 5

Great Leaders Are Decisive

*T**he very essence of leadership is that you have to have vision. You can't blow an uncertain trumpet.* – Theodore M. Hesburgh

If you've been in a situation that needed quick thinking and action, but the person in charge would not make a decision fast enough, then you know the frustration that can result from that. Decisiveness goes beyond making fast decisions for the smooth functioning of the organization; it shows your team that you're capable of leading them and that they can always trust your leadership. Research indicates that, on average, executives spend almost 40% of their time making decisions (What Is Decision Making? 2023).

If you take too much time to make critical decisions, your team may begin to lose trust in you. However, the tricky part is that you need a decent balance between being decisive and making decisions that are beneficial and effective. This chapter will teach you how to make quick and effective decisions in a business world that is fast-paced and full of uncertainty, change, and unforeseen challenges.

What Is a Decisive Leader?

One of the requisite attributes for successful leadership is decisiveness. You have to be able to stay prepared to make both well-informed and time-sensitive decisions. To achieve this, you should make an effort to seek out the appropriate and relevant information necessary to make a good decision and show understanding of the knowledge held by your team, leaders, and direct reports (Why a Decisive Leader Is a More Successful Leader, 2021).

Without decisive leaders, it would be difficult for any organization to execute plans effectively and achieve its goals. Aside from making timely decisions, decisiveness is a bit of everything that leads to realizing company goals, keeping clients and staff motivated, and staying relevant in a dynamic and fast-paced world. This means that you need to balance the cost of continued information gathering, deliberate when you should delay a decision to avoid making wrong choices, and make the decision soon enough to actually make a change. As if that's not enough, you have to be aware of competing costs in order to carefully evaluate them, and at the same time, make clear, effective, and final decisions.

To be honest, successful leadership can sometimes feel like being a magician or performing miracles, but it's attainable.

What Are the Qualities of a Decisive Leader?

The importance of being a decisive leader is not often spoken about, but its benefits can't be overemphasized. If you've dined with someone who couldn't decide what or where they wanted to eat, then you are very much aware of how frustrating that can make one feel. In that same light, I would like to challenge you to remember that feeling and imagine your team feeling that way each time you can't be decisive. I know that's not the kind of impact you want to have as a leader. Let's look at some of the ways you can benefit your organization and teams as a decisive leader (Why a Decisive Leader Is a More Successful Leader, 2021):

Responsibility and accountability: Decisive leaders are committed to doing what it takes to effectively carry out a decision. They also take responsibility and hold themselves accountable for how their decisions and outcomes affect their teams and the organization as a whole.

Confidence: Decisive leaders are confident, and when they deliver their messages, they foster confidence in others to act on their decision without second-guessing. This saves the organization time, and results produced by congruent and confident teams are more likely to be positive.

Resilience: When a decisive leader makes a decision, they are less likely to change their minds, regardless of the resistance they might face. Not every decision a leader makes is popular at first, but it's crucial to be resilient and see the decision through until it bears the kind of fruit that makes it popular. If leaders make changes and adjustments every time they are met with resistance, then decisiveness might as well be thrown out the window. This is not to promote arrogance, hastiness, or stubbornness. On the contrary, this is about trusting one's own instincts and stating them with clarity.

One thing is for sure: There are very few people willing to be led by an overthinker who constantly goes back and forth over basic decisions. Without a doubt, being a decisive leader is not only a desirable skill in business but one that helps you to maintain relevance and competitiveness in a fast-paced world.

Trust: People simply trust decisive leaders. However, this mostly refers to leaders who consider how their decisions affect their teams, their job security, and their well-being. One of the most natural things to do is gravitate toward those who have our best interests at heart. Do you want your teams to trust you, respect you, and give you their loyalty? Consider what your decisions mean for their jobs and overall well-being.

Boldness: At one point or another, you will be required to make bold decisions in the face of challenges or uncertainty. Will you allow yourself to wallow in self-doubt, fear, or anxiety, or will you rise to the occasion and take calculated risks? Leadership is definitely anything but predictable because the business world is highly dynamic. Rather than panicking, because this will just send your team into panic mode, gather the necessary information, be honest and objective when you weigh your options, and proceed to make a decision. It's part of the job; you just have to be bold enough to trust your decisions so that those under your leadership will too.

Learning: Regardless of your position and years of experience, you can make mistakes. Perhaps the decision you make ends up negatively affecting employee morale or business profits. Rather than doubting yourself, you should learn from your mistakes. You'd be mistaken to think that great leaders don't make mistakes because they do. However, great leaders rarely make the same mistake twice.

During my early days as a leader, my leadership style didn't produce the best morale and engagement in my staff. While I was considered a great problem solver and analytical thinker, some of my team members felt that I was micromanaging them. I eventually found myself working for a couple of leaders who helped me identify my leadership weaknesses and be a more effective leader.

I also had little to no patience for team members who lacked integrity and broke corporate rules, and

I often reacted disproportionately to these matters. In short, these were all mistakes I made in early leadership. However, once I learned better and more efficient ways to lead my team, I embraced them and grew from my mistakes. I'm a much better leader now, and my team's morale and engagement are better than ever.

Creating Order: Decisive leaders appreciate the importance of clarity. They seek to make their decisions as clear as possible and are willing to answer questions in a way that people understand. They avoid confusion and ambiguity by sticking to their decisions and providing a clear course of action.

Becoming More Decisive

You may be wondering whether or not you're a decisive leader. Here are some questions you can ask yourself to help you assess your ability to be a decisive leader (Espinoza, n.d.):

- Do I go out of my way to gather all the necessary information prior to making a decision?

- Do I utilize all my resources to gather the right information?

- Do I have the ability to weigh the cost of gathering information and analyzing options against that of making poor decisions?

- Do I prioritize making careful evaluations, or do I make decisions based on my intuitions alone?

- What factors necessitate an urgent decision versus one that allows me more time to think and evaluate?

Now that you can rate your level of decisiveness, the following are simple and effective ways to become more decisive. Remember, you can always learn new skills, and if you already have them, there's always room for improvement.

Identify and Gather Relevant Information

Being decisive does not necessarily mean making decisions on the go. On the contrary, it entails gathering the information necessary to reach a sound conclusion and make a good decision. To achieve this, you may need to thoroughly analyze a situation when faced with a choice, utilize available data to gather critical information and weigh your options to come up with the one best suitable for the internal and external circumstances of the organization and its employees. Moreover, being a great leader means you know that you don't always need to make decisions on your own. Rather, you can rely on the advice and expertise of your staff and those who have walked the same path. Undoubtedly, you can't make effective decisions without gathering facts.

Focus on the Right Things

As a leader, you will hardly get the chance to focus on one thing at a time since you will have to juggle different responsibilities, tasks, and obligations at the same time. Therefore, being a decisive leader isn't always about prioritizing decisions but prioritizing your leadership role. You need to know which matters are urgent, what takes priority in terms of company funds, and which tasks require more of your time and energy. Doing this will help you to feel less overwhelmed and give you the mental clarity necessary to make the right decisions and moves for you, your team, and the organization.

Be Self-Aware

There's no wrong way to approach decision-making if you're aware of your decision-making patterns or tendencies. Whether you make reason-based decisions, rely on your intuition, or utilize a decent amount of both, you need to be aware of what has worked for you in the past and vice versa. When you have this kind of awareness regarding your approach as a leader, many decisions become easy for you. You'd be surprised at how much eliminating doubt, ambiguity, and confusion will enhance the accuracy and time-effectiveness of your decision-making process.

Be Timely

Being timely when making decisions is essential for successful leadership. As a leader, it is important to have enough information to make an informed decision. However, it is also important to be mindful of the time and resources available. Leaders should strive to make decisions in a timely manner based on the most relevant and up-to-date information available. Timely decisions can help ensure that the organization is running efficiently and that employees are given the resources and support they need.

When a leader waits to gather too much information that does not impact the decision timely, it can have detrimental effects on the organization. It can lead to delays in decision-making, which can cause a decrease in productivity and employee morale. Additionally, it can lead to a lack of trust in the leader from employees and a lack of confidence in the leader's ability to make timely and informed decisions. This can lead to a decrease in the overall success of the organization.

Improving Your Decisiveness in Three Simple Ways

Remember, there's always room for growth and improvement. Whether you have a long way to go before you consider yourself a decisive leader or you're the best in the game, you can always learn new approaches to every aspect of leadership. Let's take a look at three simple steps to enhance your decisiveness:

Utilize Your Resources

Of all the resources an organization has, human resources or employees are the only unique source of competitive advantage. Your products, schedules, and approaches can always be imitated, but human beings are more complex than that. Therefore, view them as assets because they are, and they appreciate being included. Giving your team autonomy and recognition means taking note of their advice, allowing them to be an integral part of decision-making, asking them questions, actively listening, and taking their direct reports into consideration. This approach has notable benefits:

In addition to making your decision-making process more effective, it boosts employee morale and fosters loyalty. When leaders and their teams speak with one voice, they can achieve amazing results.

Prioritize Every Part of Your Role Effectively and Accordingly

There's no role or duty more important than the other when it comes to leadership. However, while every duty is crucial, they differ in their urgency and priority. When prioritizing duties, first look at the imminent problems surrounding your organization, both in its internal and external environment. You can also write down each task in terms of its urgency and relevance and work towards ticking them off, one accomplished task after the other. After doing this, you will achieve a level of mental clarity necessary to come up with decision-making guidelines that appreciate the difference in priority of each duty or issue. When it comes to making good decisions, one hardly ever has to use a one-size-fits-all approach because each business season presents different priorities. Therefore, as a leader, you need to stay flexible, adaptable, and agile.

Stay Calm Even in Times of Uncertainty

Sometimes, you have to trust that you've done everything possible with the time and resources at your disposal before making a decision. You won't always be able to collect all the information you need and get enough time to weigh your options and ask questions. This is because the business world can be extremely fast and uncertain, making any kind of decision-making very uncomfortable. Try to remain calm in a situation like this because fear and anxiety can cloud your judgment and hinder your ability to make correct and effective decisions. Remember, you're a leader for a reason, and you're more capable than you know.

The Decisive Leader

Many years of leadership taught me the importance of having a growth mindset. This gave me the freedom to try new approaches, systems, and methods for my day-to-day duties. I would gain more confidence whenever I made a quick decision that worked out effectively and positively for my team, but I would also seek to learn from my mistakes when my decisions were not so effective or productive. From all this, I learned that leadership is not a destination that you can reach but a perpetual learning curve and an opportunity to enhance your interpersonal and technical skills.

80-20 Rule

Since my nature is technical, I look at decision-making by understanding the problem I am trying to solve with my natural tendencies of critical thinking and problem-solving. A leader can make decisive decisions with the 80-20 rule and allow employees to be creative with their decision-making and critical thinking.

Because the 80-20 rule can be a valuable tool for leaders looking to make informed and timely decisions, here are the basics: The rule states that 80% of the results come from 20% of the effort. By focusing on essential aspects of a decision, a leader can make decisions quickly and efficiently while still considering the necessary information. This can help ensure that the organization is running efficiently and that employees have access to the resources and support they need.

Additionally, using the 80-20 rule can help to increase employee morale. By making timely decisions, employees will feel valued and respected as their leader is taking the time to listen to their needs and make the best decisions for the organization. Furthermore, employees will have more trust in their leader because they will be aware that the leader is making informed decisions quickly and efficiently. I found this will lead to increased employee engagement, more productivity, and a successful organization.

Chapter 6

Highly Respected Leaders Empower Others

The greatest leader is not necessarily the one who does the greatest things. He is the one that gets the people to do the greatest things. – Ronald Reagan

Leadership empowerment is a very crucial aspect of leadership because everyone appreciates feeling like they are contributing towards the company vision. You have to know what your team member's strengths are by observing their work or asking them. When you have established this, give them room to lead in their areas of strength. Of interest to mention is a Gallup study that claims about 67%

of employees whose leaders focus on their positive characteristics and strengths are engaged while only 2% whose leaders focus on their weaknesses or simply do not acknowledge their strengths are engaged (Shelton, n.d.).

When you empower your employees, you not only boost their confidence, but you also boost your confidence and trust in them. Instead of overseeing every little thing, you can empower your team and trust that they can get the job done effectively and efficiently, even without your input. This will give you more time to focus on strategic matters of the business rather than day-to-day operations.

How Is Leadership Empowerment Related to Delegation?

Empowerment and delegation are sometimes used interchangeably. While they are closely related, they are different concepts altogether. When it comes to delegation, leaders have found it useful over the years when confronted with problems. They would consider how to break down the problem into simpler and manageable tasks to assign to their staff members. However, delegation doesn't take away the planning and strategizing responsibilities from a leader because when they delegate, they have already carried out much of the legwork. They have thought the problem through, gathered the necessary information, and figured out the bigger picture. As a result, they have also broken down the problem into tasks with careful instruction on what needs to be accomplished and how (LaMarco, 2018). By the time the problem is delegated, employees are more concerned about carrying out simple and clear instructions rather than pondering what they are doing and why. Such has been the concept of delegation for many years.

However, when it comes to empowerment, the dynamics are different. While the leader still considers the bigger picture and breaks down the problem into simpler and more manageable tasks, they don't assign these tasks to their teams with instructions for them to follow without allowing room for questions. On the contrary, they explain the bigger picture, share in-depth insights, and explain what they're trying to accomplish and why. By doing so, employees know the main goal right from the beginning.

Empowerment, by its very nature, gives the employee more autonomy to make authoritative decisions when the need arises. This employee is less supervised as they carry out their task because the leader trusts their decision-making and efficiency. Overall, while delegation management revolves around giving tasks to be followed to the core, empowerment-based leadership is more about giving the front-line employee autonomy to make decisions and take authority (LaMarco, 2018).

Leadership Empowerment Defined

Leadership empowerment is the phenomenon of giving staff members the authority to make decisions, follow them up with actions, and be held responsible for outcomes. Empowerment allows employees to feel that they are a significant part of the vision, which creates buy-in. Moreover, empowerment comes in different types, namely positional, psychological, and social empowerment. Let's take a look at what each of them entails.

Positional Empowerment

This involves giving an employee a position of authority, for example, promoting them to team leader or supervisor. While this is a decent move, it's not the most effective type of empowerment. This is because there are no guarantees as to whether or not the person will be able to effectively carry out the duties that come with their new role.

Psychological Empowerment

This involves giving an employee the authority to make decisions and be held responsible for outcomes. This type of empowerment has less to do with an employee's job position and more to do with trust, which is effective because employees are more likely to trust themselves when their leaders trust them.

Social Empowerment

This is the most effective type of empowerment because it produces long-lasting results. It involves creating a conducive, supportive, and encouraging environment for employees to grow personally and professionally. This fosters loyalty and commitment.

The Significance of Leadership Empowerment

Empowered employees are more engaged, motivated, and less likely to waste resources or time. Overall, companies with empowered employees have a higher performance rate compared to their counterparts of competitors. This not only gives the company a competitive edge, but its teams are more likely to build resilience, even in times of hardship. There's no stopping a motivated employee whose loyalty lies with their organization. If, as a leader, you can foster that kind of loyalty, you will realize your goals much faster and work with much more ease and much less stress and anxiety. Together, you and your team will be unstoppable in driving profitability and growth, and your results will be exponential (Shelton, n.d.).

How to Empower Your Staff Members

Empowering your teams starts with creating an environment that encourages personal growth. Below are a few steps you can take toward achieving this:

- Encourage team members to tackle new

challenges.

- Create platforms and forums where employees can freely share ideas.

- Support employees' personal or individual professional development.

- Honor employees' time and commitments.

- Create and maintain a culture of open communication and trust.

When all is said and done, you should always remember that you can't solely lead your company or organization to success. Your leadership has a lot to do with the considerable contributions and work of your team members and their willingness to commit to the same goal (How Successful Leaders Use Empowerment to Build Trust and Excellence, n.d.). In fact, the higher you go in the organization, the more it becomes necessary for you to rely on and make full use of the diverse skill sets and talents of your team members. In an ever-changing and uncertain world, it's good to have people in your corner who are committed to doing what it takes to get results and make profits. The golden rule comes into play here: You have to do for your teams what you would have wanted your leader to do for you when you were still in their position. If you look back, you will realize that at some point, someone dared to trust you with a big responsibility and gave you the freedom to exercise autonomy and take credit or accountability for outcomes. It's because of such an opportunity that your potential was realized, and opportunities for growth opened up for you. Also, because of the level of trust given to you, you put your best foot forward and became a loyal and efficient member of the organization. That's how empowerment works for any responsible person that it's afforded or awarded to.

What If Leaders Do Not Believe in Empowerment?

Not believing in the idea of empowerment can have many detrimental effects on the leader and the organization at large. Besides getting isolated from their teams, which may affect productivity in the long run, they may become micromanagers who only believe in their ideas without listening to what other people have to say. These kinds of leaders cross-examine everyone's work and hardly praise their teams for a job well done. As a result, they make their decisions in a vacuum and become opposed to new ideas, different views, and diverse contributions.

Diversity, equality, and inclusivity become difficult to achieve in such an organization, and employees can easily become frustrated, demoralized, and resentful. This kind of leadership (which is more management than leadership) discourages critical and innovative thinking, which may affect the competitiveness and profitability of the business (How Successful Leaders Use Empowerment to Build Trust and Excellence, n.d.). Overall, empowerment isn't just a flowery or nice concept to throw around when and if you please—it's a necessity. Without it, organizations will lag behind, experience high turnover, and find it difficult to come up with new ideas and approaches to business.

Crucial Leadership Empowerment Actions You Can Take

There are simple yet effective steps you can take toward promoting empowerment in your organization. Let's get right into it (Shelton, n.d.):

Build Trust

Building trust is one of the most important steps toward empowering your employees. While it takes time and effort, you can achieve it by opening a two-way communication line between you and your team, giving feedback, and being open to receiving feedback and suggestions. The more you communicate with your team, the more you can know and trust them. It would be difficult to assign an employee a task where they have the autonomy to make decisions and be accountable for outcomes if you do not trust them.

Show Appreciation

Showing appreciation for your teams is crucial because it's a way to let them know that you value their work and contribution. As a leader, you can easily get caught up in a cycle of critically examining all the work done by your team members and giving constructive criticism. While this is okay because you're concerned about each outcome, as any mistakes may reflect negatively on your leadership skills, it's also good to show pure appreciation for what your teams do right. Sometimes you can simply appreciate their efforts and contributions, regardless of the results they yield.

To show appreciation, you can use different tactics. These include the following:

- giving verbal praise

- giving awards of recognition

- writing thank you notes

- offering incentives

There's no right or wrong way; these methods are all effective as long as you're sincere and unbiased. Additionally, each individual is different and likes to be appreciated differently. While some may appreciate being recognized in a group setting, others may prefer something more private. The key is getting to know your people and relating with them accordingly.

Collect Feedback from Your Team

Besides your duty to give feedback to your team members, it's wise to hear what they also have to say. Avoid making feedback a one-way process where employees are always on the receiving end. Without gathering feedback from employees, it would be difficult to understand their needs and concerns, which would also make it hard to provide them with support and guidance. To effectively gather feedback, make time for one-on-one meetings where you can ask them how they are doing and if there are any areas they need your support. I can't begin to explain the positive impact such meetings have had on my team members and me over the years. I was able to create a work-life balance for those struggling with boundaries, promote a growth mindset for those stuck or comfortable in the same routines, and more.

However, you will not always get time for one-on-one meetings, and understandably so. This is where collecting feedback through focus groups, surveys, and assessments comes in handy. You can fashion your assessments to measure crucial aspects like agility, trust, alignment, and passion in your team.

Create and Maintain a Universal Work Environment

A universal work environment allows everyone to feel respected and valued because it's inclusive of all staff. To create this kind of environment, you have to model inclusive behavior for your teams. If you treat a group of people as if they were superior to the other, your staff are likely to do the same. However, if you treat everyone with respect, regardless of their race, gender, religion, and more, that's the kind of environment you create and promote for everyone.

Moreover, you can easily use your company values to reinforce a universal workplace by creating a simple, descriptive, and clear set of values. After you do this, it's your responsibility as a leader to not only walk your talk but recognize and reward those able to abide by these values (Shelton, n.d.).

Encourage the Sharing of Ideas for Growth and Improvement

Whether you realize this or not, some of your team members have great ideas that can usher the organization forward. They have skill sets that you may not be aware of, and they have access to information that can make processes more efficient. However, you will not know this if you don't give them a chance. Make it a point to regularly provide forums where they can discuss what's working or not working for each department and share ideas on how to improve. You can also encourage an environment where your members are not afraid to ask questions to understand why they do what they do and allow for suggestions on how you can improve processes or approaches. After ensuring everyone understands and is on board with the vision and strategy, the best thing you can do is keep an open door for suggestions, new ideas, and opportunities.

When Empowering Employees Works and When It Doesn't

Leaders often attempt to enable their staff by granting them authority and decision-making responsibilities, sharing information, and soliciting their opinions. Numerous studies have consistently shown a significant correlation between employees feeling empowered in their jobs and increased levels of job performance, satisfaction, commitment, and loyalty to the organization. While empowering leadership is undoubtedly effective and the way to go, leaders should know when it's most effective and when that may not be the case. For example, delegating authority and decision-making will only work for a specific type of employee.

After conducting a meta-analysis of available field experiments on various leaders empowering their employees, the Harvard Business Review teams examined up to 105 studies that included data from 30,000 employees from 30 different countries (Lee et al., 2018). In this study, they analyzed whether or not there was a correlation between an empowering leadership style and enhanced job performance. They also went out of their way to test if this was the case for various performance types, including routine task performance, creativity, and organizational citizenship behavior.

As if this wasn't enough, this experiment left nothing to chance in this matter as they also tested different mechanisms to try and explain why the empowering leadership style was effective in enhancing performance. One of the questions asked to try and reach a conclusion was whether the results of leadership empowerment (increased job performance) resulted from enhanced feelings of trust in one's leader or increased feelings of empowerment. Finally, they also dug deeper into whether or not leadership empowerment enhanced employee job performance universally or across various cultures, levels of experience, and industries.

The Harvard Business Review Analysis came up with different results from their analysis. The first one was the fact that empowering leaders were more effective or successful at influencing positive employee behavior like citizenship and creativity. Employee citizenship behavior refers to behavior that doesn't normally come with recognition or reward, for example, helping team members or attending functions that are not mandatory.

The second conclusion was that leaders who empower their employees are more likely to gain their trust compared to those who do not exercise leadership empowerment. Thirdly, they found that leaders who empowered their staff had more success at influencing and improving employee performance in Eastern cultures compared to Western ones, and they had more impact on staff members who had less experience in their organization compared to more experienced ones (Lee et al., 2018).

Empowering Leaders Had More Creative and Helpful/Engaged Employees

Moreover, the same meta-analysis made a comparison of the effects of leaders who were regarded and rated more empowering by their direct reports compared to their counterparts. Leaders who were seen as more empowering tended to delegate authority to their employees, request their input, and promote autonomous decision-making. They were also more likely to have employees who were rated as highly creative and excellent organizational citizens by either their leader or coworkers. In particular, this style of leadership appears to stimulate employees to generate original ideas and devise innovative methods of doing things, as well as to assist others in the workplace, take on additional assignments, and demonstrate a willingness to support their organization beyond their official duties (Lee et al., 2018).

Harvard Business Review states that these effects were a result of two different psychological processes. First, employees who regarded their leaders as empowering also felt empowered in their respective jobs as they experienced a significant sense of autonomy or control in their jobs. As a result of being empowered, they also experienced a great sense of meaning in their jobs and felt that it aligned with their personal values. Overall, they believed they could make a difference and felt confident in their abilities. These feelings accounted for their boost in creativity and citizenship behavior. When leaders empower their employees, they reap amazing benefits, both in the present and future. Their employees are more likely to be powerful, confident, and committed to getting results and reaching goals. Because they have the freedom to share new ideas, methods, and perspectives, they are more likely to be innovative.

Secondly, empowering leaders gained their employees' trust. Because employees had more faith in their leaders, they were more willing to go the extra mile for their jobs without feeling exploited or taken advantage of. It's crucial for you to know that leadership empowerment is not merely about giving employees more responsibilities and freedom to make decisions. Some might even interpret that as an attempt to avoid doing the work yourself and take advantage of subordinates.

Therefore, for leadership empowerment to be effective, it should be accompanied by an effort to mentor one's employees and support their growth. When you do this, you're more likely to build trust. Overall, just like psychological empowerment, the trust leaders build with their teams when they mentor them and support their growth is responsible for improved creativity and citizenship in the same employees. When employees trust their leaders, they feel safer and less uncertain. Consequently, they are more likely to tackle challenges and take on more risks without feelings of vulnerability getting in the way.

Feeling Empowered Won't Always Enhance Routine Task Performance

Harvard Business Review states that their research portrayed that effective leaders who empowered their teams were associated with positive job performance in regard to routine and essential job duties, but the difference from non-empowering leaders was negligible (Lee et al., 2018). Additionally, their findings showed a significant level of variability in the effectiveness of empowerment approaches. In some cases, leaders who aimed to empower their employees actually had a detrimental impact. For example, one study in their analysis showed that empowering leaders who tried to offer additional responsibilities and challenges at work caused excessive stress for their employees. However, leaders who were successful in empowering their employees and achieving improved performance on routine tasks were those who prioritized building strong relationships with their team members and fostering trust.

Once again, the findings confirmed that the impact of empowering leadership depends on employees' perceptions of their leader's actions. Employees may interpret increased autonomy or participatory decision-making as evidence that their leader has faith in their abilities and is encouraging their personal and professional growth. Alternatively, they may perceive these actions as indications that their leader is unable to lead effectively and is avoiding making tough choices. In this scenario, employees may feel confused and frustrated, leading to a subpar performance on routine tasks. Therefore, it is crucial for leaders to strike a balance when empowering their employees and avoid adding excessive pressure or creating uncertainty.

Understanding employees' expectations is crucial. Current research has highlighted that employees hold specific expectations regarding how leaders should empower them. If leaders' attempts to empower their subordinates do not align with their expectations, such as granting too much or too little autonomy and decision-making responsibility, subordinates may perceive these behaviors negatively. Therefore, it is vital for leaders to take into account their subordinates' expectations and tailor their empowering strategies accordingly to achieve optimal outcomes.

The Empowering Leader

The empowering leader goes beyond delegating tasks and giving decision-making authority to their employees. This leader recognizes the importance of building trust and lasting relations with their teams so that they can know how best to support their dreams and provide mentorship.

Therefore, to adopt leadership empowerment effectively, it's crucial to recognize that when there is no trust, your efforts to empower others can be interpreted as avoiding responsibility, weakness, or exploitation. Just like everything in life, leadership empowerment works under the right circumstances.

When you do it right, you will be able to enhance performance, foster commitment, and overall boost your organization's return on investment. The universal truth is that leaders who empower their teams are more effective in enhancing employee performance compared to those who don't.

Chapter 7

Effective Leaders Are Adaptable

The ability to adapt quickly is key to any successful leader. – Richard Branson

Adapting to constant change is not a new concept for organizations and their leaders. With disruptions caused by technological and digital advancements, shifts in cultural, market, and consumer trends, and growing concern for non-commercial business outcomes, such as environmental sustainability and social responsibility, leaders have had to foster innovation and stay ahead of the ever-evolving landscape. However, the COVID-19 pandemic has posed a serious challenge to the survival of all organizations, causing many to reconsider their business strategies. In 2019, adaptability was recognized as the most desirable skill (Why Adaptability Is a Critical Capability for Future

Leadership, 2020). Yet, in order to effectively lead their people and organizations, adaptability in leaders is no longer a desirable trait; it is essential for success both now and in the future.

What Makes an Adaptable Leader?

An adaptable leader is not stuck in their processes, approaches, and ideas. Rather, they are flexible and able to change their behavior in response to situational changes. An adaptable leader is a desirable leader because not only are they capable of flexibility, but they are ready to keep pushing on when things don't go according to plan and learn from their mistakes. This leader isn't afraid to innovate and try new things, and their growth mindset makes it easy for them to bounce back from their failures.

The universal fact of business, especially in today's fast-paced world, is that there's no approach, ideology, or solution to doing business that is one-size-fits-all. With different contexts, internal and external environments, and unforeseen changes, business leaders need to stay agile so that they can respond appropriately to various business contexts. When leaders are adaptable, they are more strategically empowering to their teams, and their organizations are able to maintain profitability through different business scenarios.

What Is Adaptability in the Workplace?

Workplace adaptability entails effectively responding to various scenarios and challenges that arise in the workplace. It involves more than simply being flexible. Individuals with adaptability skills cultivate specific sets of skills, procedures, and structures that enable them to handle diverse situations promptly and proficiently.

By acquiring adaptability skills, you can effectively respond to new situations, roles, projects, and clients in your workplace. As you enhance your adaptability, you will be better equipped to tackle any changes that may occur.

The Three Types of Adaptability Skills

There are three categories that the Center for Creative Leadership uses to classify adaptability skills (Leading Effectively Staff, 2021):

Cognitive Adaptability

With cognitive adaptability, you can evaluate various potential scenarios and prepare for different outcomes. While developing cognitive adaptability does not ensure that you will make the right decision, it assists in organizing your thoughts while making decisions.

Emotional Adaptability

While it may seem cliche, it's reasonable to assume that every colleague has a unique approach, thought process, and individuality. Emotional adaptability skills enable you to acknowledge and accept these differences, allowing you to connect with diverse personalities, especially those that differ from your own.

Personality Adaptability

An adaptable personality enables you to perceive a situation for what it currently is and what it can potentially become. When confronted with a challenge, you possess the ability to assess the whole situation, recognize flaws, and identify opportunities. This blend of realism and optimism is valuable in responding to any situation.

How Can Leaders Develop Adaptability?

Leaders can develop adaptability in many different ways. Let's have a look at some of the most effective ones (Why Adaptability Is a Critical Capability for Future Leadership, 2020):

Develop an Adaptive Mindset

Having a growth mindset really comes into play here. Great leaders have the distinct ability to view challenges as opportunities to learn. With each new challenge you face in your role lies an opportunity to innovate. This is when you learn new methods of doing business, problem-solving skills, and more. The COVID-19 pandemic is a good example. Because of it, many businesses were threatened, but they soon found out that most of their operations could be done efficiently from home. Rather than lagging behind and losing profits, businesses adopted remote working, and all of a sudden, meetings that normally took hours to organize and facilitate could be done on Zoom with participants at different ends of the country or world, which became the order of the day.

Therefore, when you face challenges, rather than being pessimistic and drowning in frustration, challenge your perception of the situation and your assumptions around success. When you do this, you will not only learn from the experience but use that experience to drive improvements for future changes or challenges.

Seek Different or Diverse Opinions

The most challenging and perhaps even interesting thing about a rapidly changing business world is that people who were regarded as experts may no longer be the most knowledgeable in their areas of work—leadership is not an exception. Recognizing this fact will give you the modesty you need to seek out different opinions in order to figure out the best possible approach or solution to your problems. The truth is that whether you have many years of leadership experience or are very educated in that field, there are areas you may require help. Experience or education cannot anticipate some of the changes the future throws at businesses. If you think about it, who could have possibly anticipated the COVID-19 pandemic and a world shutdown?

Moreover, seeking diverse opinions will help you challenge confirmation bias. This refers to the inclination to exaggerate the significance of the information that supports one's preexisting beliefs and to underestimate the importance of information that contradicts one's perspectives. Leaders who hold on to confirmation bias are often reluctant to innovate, consider differing perspectives, and expose their teams to new approaches. This type of leader can by no means be called an adaptive leader, and unfortunately, they can be restricted in their thinking and, as a result, limit their teams, outcomes, and organizations. To combat this problem, seek to learn from others within your organization or otherwise, even when their ideas are completely different from yours. You can also take inspiration from those excelling and adjusting well to their changing business environment. Leaders know a great deal, but they can also benefit tremendously from learning from others.

Create and Maintain Psychological Safety

Leaders cannot reap the benefits of diverse perspectives if they don't give their employees a safe environment to express *their opinions*, *be inventive*, and *even make mistakes.*

You shouldn't wait for the business world to change to start prioritizing your team member's opinions. Rather, you should always maintain a psychologically safe environment for your teams, where they don't have to walk on eggshells around you, but feel free to communicate views that are different from yours without fearing for their jobs or positions. Make it a point to cultivate an atmosphere of learning from setbacks by admitting your own mistakes and sharing the lessons learned with your team members.

Be Emotionally Intelligent and Agile

Let's face it. Adaptability is a nice and effective concept, but it doesn't always come easy. Some situations will cause you stress and frustration, and if you're not careful, you won't be able to tackle them logically and effectively because your fear may cloud your judgment. This is why it's crucial for leaders to develop emotional intelligence; it enables them to be aware of their emotions and to control them while also enhancing their emotional agility (the skill of effectively handling, rather than repressing, thoughts and emotions).

When you have emotional agility, you experience decreased levels of stress, heightened creativity, and increased job proficiency. By being aware of your emotion and knowing and exploring your underlying triggers, you can prevent undesirable consequences and avoid depleting your cognitive resources. Overall, your ability to withstand adversity and bounce back promptly from setbacks will be enhanced.

Assessing Adaptability in Leaders

As we navigate the current landscape of what is being called the "new normal," we find ourselves in an environment marked by constant change and instability, which is likely to persist and further evolve in the future. The rate of change impacting organizations is only going to accelerate, thereby making it increasingly imperative for leaders to be able to adapt to the new challenges facing their organizations.

Leaders who wish to assess their own adaptability can start by reflecting on their past experiences and how they have dealt with change. They should consider their response to unexpected challenges and their ability to adjust to changing circumstances. One way to evaluate adaptability is to analyze how you approach new situations. Are you open to new ideas and receptive to feedback, or do you cling to old ways of doing things? Are you willing to experiment with new methods and strategies, or do you prefer to stick to tried-and-true approaches?

Another important factor to consider is how you handle setbacks and failures. Are you quick to blame others, or do you take responsibility for your actions and learn from your mistakes? Do you bounce back quickly from setbacks and maintain a positive attitude, or do you become discouraged and give up easily?

You can also assess your adaptability by seeking feedback from others, such as colleagues, mentors, or coaches. This can provide valuable insights into areas where you may need to improve and help you identify new opportunities for growth. Ultimately, you should know that leaders who are adaptable are able to navigate change and uncertainty with confidence and resilience and are better equipped to lead their organizations through periods of transition and transformation. Be that leader!

Adapting to Change Requires Flexibility

Give your leadership role the best shot by becoming flexible and learning to embrace, accept, and lead through change. If you're wondering how to do this, just hang on tight and keep reading. Let's get started.

Becoming a More Flexible Leader

Leaders worldwide are encountering challenges and change now more than ever. At every turn, they are presented with new circumstances, challenges, and uncertainties. What do they do, and where do they start, especially with everyone looking to them for solutions? The unforeseen COVID-19 challenge, for example, saw too many changes within the business sector. Since then, jobs have been shrinking, morphing, and even disappearing. Everything surrounding the workplace dynamic is changing: Technology, teammates, and coworkers are all changing at a rapid pace to meet the new demands. Nowadays, many employees value the freedom to work from any location as long as they can accomplish their tasks. Failing to provide this flexibility can make it harder to recruit and retain employees.

However, with the rollout of vaccines and a gradual return to in-person work, there has now been a new set of norms and challenges to face. It is crucial for leaders to be adaptable, as change is a constant and inevitable aspect of business success. Research confirms that adaptability is imperative for leaders. It involves having a range of behaviors readily available to shift and experiment as circumstances change. Let's take a look at what adapting to change may entail (Leading Effectively Staff, 2021):

- adapting to various external challenges confronting the organization

- having a positive attitude toward change

- adjusting your leadership style to suit external and internal changes

- being open to revising your plans and strategizing

- actively listening to your team member's concerns and views during change

Unfortunately, the inability to adapt can lead to career derailment. This is because when leaders are inflexible, they can impede the adaptability of their colleagues in the workplace. Additionally, they can also hinder new initiatives, which is not good for any kind of business. Resistance to change can undermine crucial projects or system-wide implementation, resulting in setbacks in progress and also creating anxiety and negative emotions among employees and sometimes even clients. The enthusiasm, cooperation, morale, and creativity of employees can be compromised, making it more challenging to manage the business or organization.

Do You Consider Yourself a Flexible Leader? How Well Would You Say You Adapt to Change?

How do you typically respond to change at a personal level? Do you

- embrace the change as a positive development?

- view the change as a chance to seize new opportunities?

- adjust your plans to fit the new circumstances?

- rapidly learn new technology, terminology, and procedures?

- lead by example and champion the change?

- consider the concerns and perspectives of others?

- evaluate your strengths and weaknesses with honesty?

- acknowledge personal errors, learn from them, and move forward?

- maintain an optimistic outlook?

It's perfectly normal if you don't identify with some or any of the listed responses. Change can be challenging, and everyone responds to it differently. It's okay to feel anxious or uncertain about the unknown. The important thing is to acknowledge your feelings and work on finding strategies to help you navigate through change. With time and practice, you can develop your own personal approach to change that works for you.

In order to navigate change within your organization, industry, or profession, it's important to take responsibility for leading yourself through the transition process. This involves finding ways to ground yourself during potentially difficult times, recognizing the impact of the change on yourself, and understanding how your behavior affects others.

If you are leading the change, it's essential to keep in mind that every employee wants answers to four core questions:

1. What is happening?

2. Why is it happening?

3. How will this affect me and my job?

4. What is the plan for getting there?

By being proactive and addressing these questions before employees ask, you can help to alleviate anxiety and build trust in the change process. Keep the lines of communication open, be transparent about the reasons behind the change, and provide clear guidance on what employees can expect during the transition. Remember to listen to feedback and adjust the plan as necessary to ensure a successful outcome for everyone involved.

The Adaptable Leader

The adaptable leader can adjust their leadership style and strategies to meet the needs of a changing organization or environment. They are proactive, flexible, and responsive to changing circumstances and are able to navigate uncertainty and ambiguity.

This leader has a growth mindset and is committed to ongoing learning and development.

In times of change, the adaptable leader can be crucial for an organization's survival. They can lead the organization through difficult transitions, such as mergers or downsizing, by maintaining a clear vision and communicating effectively with employees. They are able to assess the risks and opportunities associated with change and take action accordingly. This leader is also able to inspire their teams to embrace change and work together to achieve shared goals. They build trust and foster a culture of openness and innovation, encouraging employees to think creatively and take risks.

Overall, the adaptable leader is an essential asset for any organization in times of change. They can help the organization navigate challenges, seize opportunities, and thrive in a constantly evolving environment.

Chapter 8

Highly Respected Leaders Have Confidence in Themselves and Others

The task of the leader is to get his people from where they are to where they have not been.
– Henry Kissinger

If you've ever been asked to complete a task and the person in charge did not have confidence in you or themselves, you know how demotivating that can be. Leaders need to have confidence in themselves first and then in their teams. Gartner conducted a global survey of 4,000 employees, which revealed that only 50% of employees believe their team leader efficiently establishes a future vision for the team. Furthermore, the survey indicates a more concerning issue, with just 50% of over 2,800 leaders surveyed claiming they possess the necessary skills to lead their organization effectively in the future (Baker, 2019).

However, there's a strong interdependence on leadership confidence and successful outcomes. We are going to explore that in this chapter. Let's get right into it.

The Vital Link Between Leadership and Confidence

Leadership, just like any other position of influence, is built on a foundation of confidence. Undoubtedly, it is possible to train a leader for success in various aspects of leadership like problem-solving, decision-making, communication, coaching, mentoring, and accountability, but without self-belief, their leadership will remain superficial. Therefore, it is crucial for leaders to believe in themselves because, without self-confidence, they cannot run the organization efficiently. Additionally, leaders must first convince themselves that they have the necessary qualities to lead before they can convince others. Overall, the first step in gaining followers is to sell yourself on your own confidence as a leader. Without this, acquiring followers will be an impossible or unattainable task.

According to lifelong entrepreneur Francisco Dao, self-confidence is requisite for the growth of leadership. Attempting to teach leadership without first creating confidence is similar to building a house with sand as the foundation. While it may have a beautiful coat of paint, it will ultimately shake (Stark, 2014).

It's human nature to prefer working with leaders who have a healthy dose of confidence and humility. Additionally, people tend to trust confident leaders compared to their counterparts. This means working with a confident leader assures you of their competence, and you're more likely to follow their lead without any hesitation.

Leaders usually demonstrate the following traits when they display confidence (Stark, 2014):

Happiness: Confident leaders have a "can-do" attitude, regardless of the challenges they might face. They maintain a positive attitude about their roles and teams, and as a result, they create an atmosphere for their teams to feel relaxed and motivated to do their jobs.

Ability to build better relationships: Leaders with confidence tend to treat others with respect. Because they are happy with themselves and have a healthy mindset, they coexist peacefully with others. As a result, they build and maintain strong bonds with their teams.

Motivation and drive: They believe in their ability to drive company goals and enhance profits. Leaders with confidence are motivated to realize or accomplish their goals. Because of this, they are a good influence on their teams because they effectively lead by example.

Ability to take risks: Leaders with confidence can take calculated risks. You have probably already had to make a decision on the go without being afforded time to deliberate and gather information. That's just part of leadership. Sometimes it's necessary to take risks and usher the organization forward or learn from your mistakes.

Laughter: These leaders have the ability to find humor in any situation and are consequently able to solve problems with so much ease.

Ability to recognize success: They can recognize success in others and compliment or reward it accordingly so as to reinforce the behavior that led to it. They are also able to acknowledge their own success and are not uncomfortable being complimented or rewarded for it.

Ability to receive feedback: They don't perceive themselves as superior beings who know it all. Instead, they are happy to receive feedback from their teams and put other people's ideas into action. As a result, they are able to grow even more because their teams constantly go to them with ideas for improvement.

Independent thinking: Although they embrace feedback, they are also independent thinkers who stand by their word. Consequently, their words and actions match, and people find it easier to trust them.

Finally, it's important to keep in mind that despite not making the headlines of leadership prerequisites, confidence is actually the defining factor that distinguishes average leaders from great ones. One may even argue that it's an asset that is even more valuable than skill, knowledge, or experience. Without confidence, you can't be a decisive leader, and if that's not enough, you will find it challenging to show authority when leading meetings, communicate effectively, or accept feedback. Leaders should not doubt their abilities because when they do, they begin to second-guess every choice they make and become defensive when challenged. In the end, a lack of confidence can leave you without one crucial element of leadership: followers (Stark, 2014).

I strongly urge every leader to work on developing their confidence. People are more likely to trust and have confidence in leaders who believe in their capabilities. If you want your teams to invest their time and energy in their jobs and be loyal to the organization, you have to show them that you're confident in the vision and your ability to bring it to fruition.

How Leaders Can Improve Their Self-Confidence

A leader with self-confidence is an asset to the organization, both in the present and future. This leader looks positively ahead and knows that they will continue getting results in the future, regardless of their internal or external circumstances. They also take calculated risks to help them realize their personal and organizational goals. Overall, without confidence, it's difficult to put all the attributes this book talks about into action. Let's take a look at how you can boost your self-confidence and become an effective leader (Daskal, n.d.):

Confront and overcome your self-doubt: Self-doubt is nothing to be ashamed of—we all have it. Everyone has an inner voice constantly whispering negative things to them and inflicting doubt. However, you have to recognize this voice and decide not to entertain it. Try to not only identify this voice but to seek out its origins so that you can effectively silence it.

Turn your self-doubt into confidence: Did you know that it's possible to leverage your self-doubt? It's normal to feel uncertain, but when this happens, rather than focusing on that, try shifting your attention to what you're knowledgeable about, skilled in, and proficient at. You can easily set aside any self-doubt by concentrating on your competencies and abilities. The plus side to doing this is that you will discover the confidence you require along the way.

Eliminate your triggers: Work on recognizing your negative thinking patterns. Doing this will help you avoid spending time in environments or situations that can trigger you into feeling inadequate or incompetent. Triggers take many different forms: people, places, or circumstances that leave you doubting your value and worth.

As previously mentioned, in my early days as a leader, I made the mistake of attempting to create the best possible work environment in the wrong manner. I had certain triggers, such as employees who failed to adhere to corporate regulations or prioritize impact, those who refused to assist others, and individuals lacking integrity. Consequently, I would react excessively to these issues compared to someone who made an honest mistake with similar consequences, to whom I would have been more lenient. However, I sought guidance from other leaders or business partners with different styles to help me keep things in perspective. I would inquire directly if my position seemed reasonable or if they had alternative suggestions for approaching the issue. This approach helped me manage my response to individuals, enabling me to pause and re-evaluate when I encountered one of my triggers.

I encourage you to make it a point to surround yourself with individuals and experiences that uplift and inspire you. Additionally, you can seek out activities that promote personal growth and development. Positive self-talk also comes into play here; it will help you reinforce your confidence and self-belief. Leaders have enough burdens, and prioritizing their mental health is key to making sure they give the best version of themselves to their teams and jobs.

Know your talents: It helps to focus on your strengths. To do this, work on recognizing what you're best at and appreciate your talents. Avoid comparing yourself with other people so that you don't fall prey to imposter syndrome. When you focus on what you're not good at, you may fail to realize and acknowledge your wins. However, if you celebrate your strengths, it will be easier to work on perfecting your skills where you lack them.

Grow from mistakes: It's important to keep in mind that perfection is unattainable, and every individual, no matter how confident, has insecurities and flaws. Rather than being too hard on yourself when you make errors, you should give yourself room to make mistakes. People who get everything right are not trying new methods of doing things or challenging themselves to get outside their comfort zone. This is called a fixed mindset, and leaders should refrain from it.

Moreover, when you make mistakes, they should not shake your confidence and lead you to doubt your capabilities. Instead, treat these mistakes as growth opportunities. When you accept your flaws and learn from your mistakes, you will not only grow your confidence, but you will become a better leader as you will adopt more efficient methods of achieving results along the way.

Be around individuals who have faith in your abilities and potential: Be around people who view you in a positive light. Doing so is not only empowering, but it helps you build unwavering confidence in your abilities and potential. Be intentional about cultivating and maintaining connections with such people. They will uplift, inspire, and overall help you view the world through an optimistic lens.

Honor your worth: Contrary to popular belief, taking pride in yourself doesn't negate humanity. It's possible to take pride in oneself without compromising humility. Being proud of yourself and your accomplishments helps you to value your unique qualities. Additionally, this simple act will serve as a powerful motivator in times of change or unforeseen challenges.

However, you should strive to keep a healthy balance between self-pride and humility so that you can recognize that everyone has areas for growth and improvement. Dare to be kind to yourself and celebrate your hard work, unique qualities, lessons, and wins. Be proud of how far you have come and your efforts to get there.

Lead from within: When you lack confidence, even your influence is compromised. Find the attributes that make you proud of who you are and work on your shortcomings. Remember that no one has it all figured out.

Why Leaders Need to Be Confident

Confidence should be considered a requisite ingredient for leadership. Let's dive into why this trait is so crucial for every leader (Reddy, n.d.):

Confident Leaders Have Vision and Courage

Confident leaders are effective. They possess a clear vision of the direction they wish to take and they are driven to get there. They formulate well-defined plans that align with their vision and effectively get buy-in and motivate their team to work towards it.

Moreover, confidence plays a significant role in a leader's ability to easily navigate challenging situations with courage and determination. In order to guide their team members towards success, a leader must be self-assured and courageous enough to make difficult decisions, trust their instincts, and take decisive action.

Without courage, a leader may struggle to inspire trust and may hesitate to take necessary risks. I can't emphasize this enough: Courage is an essential component of leadership. Not only does it enable individuals to lead with conviction and take bold actions that lead to positive outcomes, but it helps them guide their team toward success.

Confident Leaders Communicate Effectively

Confident leaders know the importance of choosing their words carefully and wisely. When they address their teams, their language inspires, motivates, and fosters a positive reaction from their teams. Additionally, their intentions are always to pursue positive outcomes when they communicate. They don't focus on discouraging their teams and pointing out their shortfalls without giving constructive feedback. Not only do they effectively convey their message through their words but with gestures, tone of voice, and facial expressions.

These leaders remain calm and composed during trying business times, which has a positive and calming effect on their teams.

They Are Self-Assured

A leader who possesses self-confidence has an unwavering belief in their capabilities, choices, and actions. They are free from insecurities at every level, which allows them to trust that their leadership skills will guide their team successfully. Such leaders are not easily swayed by negativity or the comments of critics as they are aware of their own effectiveness.

They Make Others Feel Significant

A leader who exudes self-confidence not only feels significant themselves but also tends to have the same effect on others; their teams draw confidence from them and feel confident themselves. This is because confident leaders constantly seek to empower their teams by entrusting them with responsibility and allowing them to take credit for them. A truly confident and effective leader recognizes the importance of their team and acts with consideration towards them. Who wouldn't thrive and shine under such leadership or mentorship? Their teams feel valued and acknowledged for every successfully completed task.

They Are Satisfied with Their Roles

When a leader exudes confidence, they can't help but feel a sense of happiness in leading and guiding others. This is in spite of the risks they might have to take or the challenges they may face. Consequently, their positive attitude translates into self-motivation and an unshakeable drive to tackle any task that comes their way with a can-do attitude. The good thing about such leaders is that they are not only driven, but they inspire their teams to approach their work with the same drive and zeal. They are constantly creating a culture of optimism and positivity. Overall, their team members feel valued and pleased to work under the leadership of such a positive influence.

They Have Ambition

Confident leaders are inherently ambitious and self-motivated. They constantly set new goals for themselves and their team, and therefore, they are never stuck in a comfort zone. Hard work is important to them, and they don't just expect it from others; they are willing to get their own hands dirty and get work done. Every task, regardless of size, is crucial to them. As a result, every task they do, big or small, plays a huge role in achieving overall company goals. Their mindset puts the company image in a positive light because their teams are dedicated to achieving excellent results and approach each task with the utmost devotion and care. Ultimately, confident leaders not only foster a culture of success within the company but also inspire their team members to grow, both personally and professionally.

They Have Strong Conflict Resolution Skills

Confident leaders know how to maintain peaceful industrial relations. This is because they are able to effectively manage and resolve conflicts that may arise in a variety of situations. Besides refraining from any kind of bias or favoritism, they are determined and have the skills to identify the root cause of the conflict and develop necessary strategies to address it in a fair and productive manner. Additionally, such leaders remain calm and composed in uncomfortable or tense situations, effectively communicate their thoughts or ideas, and actively listen to their team members' perspectives. Overall, their strong conflict-resolution skills enable them to build and maintain positive relationships and promote a harmonious work environment.

They Are Calm

One of the most effective ways to become a highly respected leader is by building and maintaining a good reputation. It's important for leaders to have the ability to remain calm during a storm, and confident leaders have this ability.

They are fully aware of the fact that maintaining a sense of calmness, regardless of the situation, is important; therefore, they try not to become frustrated or troubled. They know that frustration will not yield positive results. In situations where things have gone awry, anxiety is never the answer or an effective tool for tackling the issue. Confident leaders understand this and are able to maintain their cool, relying on their ability to overcome obstacles to guide them through. Such an approach gives them time to properly and adequately evaluate the situation, understand it without feeling frightened, and make a quick and informed decision. Overall, remaining calm in difficult situations is a key trait of a confident leader, and it makes a world of difference where outcomes are concerned.

They Correct Mistakes

Confident leaders don't wallow in self-pity and frustration when they make mistakes. Because they don't hold themselves to an unattainable standard, they can easily move on and be proactive in seeking solutions and growing from their blunders, as well as extend the same grace to their teams when they also make blunders.

Having confidence in themselves helps them to accept responsibility for their erroneous decisions and actively seek solutions or help to rectify them. When leaders are willing to admit their faults, their teams are inspired to do the same. This can easily create an environment of openness, accountability, and transparency.

They Are Not Arrogant

Confident leaders are not arrogant because they know that arrogance can negatively affect team dynamics and productivity. They do their best to strike a balance between confidence and humility so that they can use their influence to benefit the company without demoralizing their employees.

Leaders with arrogance and a domineering personality can easily instill fear and resentment in their teams and, as a result, hinder creativity and collaboration. However, a confident leader who is considerate and empowers their team is able to build and maintain a positive work environment and inspire productivity.

The Leader with Confidence

A leader who has confidence in themselves and others can trust their own abilities and those of their team members. They believe in their team's potential and empower them to take ownership of their work, make decisions, and contribute to the overall success of the organization. This type of leader fosters a culture of accountability and responsibility, allowing team members to take risks and learn from their mistakes. They also provide support, guidance, and resources to their team members to help them achieve their goals. A leader with confidence in themselves and others creates a positive and motivating work environment where team members feel valued and appreciated and are encouraged to develop their skills and knowledge.

Chapter 9

Highly Effective Leaders Are Collaborative

L *eadership is about creating an environment in which people can collaborate and work together to achieve great things.* – Simon Sinek

In today's modern age, the collaborative leadership style is considered one of the most effective management approaches. It seeks to unite leaders, managers, and staff towards a common goal by breaking down hierarchical structures and distributing responsibilities across the workforce. In fact, collaboration is an essential aspect of many jobs in the United States, and more than 50% of workers consider it a crucial part of their work. Additionally, teamwork and collaboration are highly valued by around 75% of employees, and employers have recognized this trend by using online collaboration tools and social media to communicate with their staff.

Additionally, a lack of collaboration has been identified by 86% of employees in leadership positions as the leading cause of workplace failures. On the other hand, companies that prioritize collaboration and communication have been found to reduce employee turnover rates by 50%. Engaging in collaboration at work also leads to a higher job satisfaction rate, with employees being, on average, 17% more satisfied with their job. Over the last two decades, workplace collaboration has increased by at least 50%, emphasizing the importance of collaboration in today's workplaces (Boskamp, 2023).

Collaborative Leaders Bring Diverse People Together

While diversity in the workplace is crucial for fostering true inclusivity within organizations, simply hiring people from diverse backgrounds is not enough. The question then becomes: How can companies and platforms achieve true inclusion? The answer lies in exceptional leadership that transcends differences in ethnicity, religion, age, gender, or sexual orientation and instead focuses on treating all individuals as human beings. Such leaders can cultivate a positive work environment where individuals from diverse backgrounds feel welcomed and valued. However, before exploring the mechanisms by which leaders bring people together, it is important to first understand why people often feel disconnected from one another. Read on to discover the answers to these questions (Ziegler, 2022-a).

What Is the Significance of Diversity and Inclusion in the Workplace?

While state laws may require companies and organizations to prioritize diversity and inclusion in their hiring practices, there are numerous other benefits to fostering inclusive environments within organizations. Although external pressure may be a catalyst for this change, the advantages of such an approach are numerous. Below are some reasons why diverse and inclusive environments are more effective (Ziegler, 2022-a):

Enhanced Productivity and Revenue Growth

Organizations that are structurally diverse and inclusive in their leadership behavior often achieve success in the market. By prioritizing these values, companies can cultivate a positive reputation and develop a compassionate brand image. In a world where brand image is as crucial to revenue as the quality of the product or service offered, it is essential to project an inclusive and caring approach.

Enhanced Employee Satisfaction

When employees are happy and fulfilled in their work, they are better able to perform to their fullest potential and make valuable contributions to the company's bottom line. In contrast, organizations that perpetuate prejudice, discrimination, and favoritism may find that only some employees are motivated to excel while others may simply do the bare minimum required to get by. Around 83% of employees depend on technology to collaborate while approximately 75% of them consider teamwork and collaboration significant (Dimovski, 2023).

By fostering an inclusive environment that welcomes people from diverse backgrounds, companies can inspire all employees to give their all and work towards achieving positive results. This, in turn, can lead to increased productivity, higher levels of job satisfaction, and, eventually, greater revenue for the company.

Better Employee Retention

It is a widely recognized fact that companies that prioritize the well-being and job satisfaction of their employees tend to enjoy higher levels of employee retention. When employees feel valued, respected, and supported, they are more likely to form a strong bond with the company and remain committed for the long term, even if they may not receive the highest compensation.

Furthermore, prioritizing employee well-being can also have a positive impact on overall team morale and productivity. Happy employees are often more engaged and motivated in their work, leading to increased levels of creativity, innovation, and collaboration. This, in turn, can result in better performance, higher-quality output, and, eventually, greater success for the company.

Reduced Legal Troubles

While it is important to prioritize inclusivity for its own sake, it is worth noting that there are also legal benefits to fostering a diverse and equitable workplace culture. When companies engage in discriminatory behavior, they open themselves up to a wide range of legal disputes and complaints from employees.

These problems can be particularly acute in cases where individuals feel that they have been unfairly treated in hiring or firing decisions. By contrast, inclusive workplaces are less likely to face these types of legal challenges, allowing companies to focus their energies on achieving their broader organizational goals.

How Can Collaborative Leaders Bring People Together?

Let's take a look at how collaborative leaders can effectively bring people together (Ziegler, 2022-a):

Emphasize Inclusive Behavior, Not Just Structural Changes

While structural changes such as diversity policies and equity measures are certainly important in promoting inclusivity, they are only the beginning. To truly create a workplace culture that is welcoming and supportive of everyone, leaders must focus on driving behavioral changes across their organizations.

This can begin with cultivating a leadership style that is characterized by openness, respect, and a commitment to inclusivity. Leaders must make a concerted effort to build strong relationships with their team members, ensuring that every individual feels valued, heard, and supported, regardless of their background or identity.

In addition to these interpersonal efforts, leaders must also prioritize the implementation of equity policies and other structural changes that promote inclusivity. However, these measures must be more than just surface-level gestures; they must be fully integrated into the company's values and culture and consistently upheld in practice.

By combining structural changes with behavioral shifts, leaders can create a workplace culture that is truly inclusive and supportive of all team members, leading to increased morale, productivity, and overall success.

Offering Employees Regular Opportunities to Socialize and Interact

Many companies prioritize results and revenues above all else, often at the expense of team-building exercises. However, this approach can be counterproductive to fostering a positive work environment. Successful startups have recognized the importance of team-building and prioritized activities and trips that allow employees to connect and bond outside of the office.

Leaders who aim to create a welcoming and inclusive workplace should provide frequent opportunities for employees to intermingle and develop lifelong connections. These activities bring people from diverse backgrounds together and allow them to break down barriers and reduce prejudices and biases.

Evaluate and Eradicate Personal Biases

Unconscious bias, also referred to as implicit bias, encompasses the attitudes or stereotypes that impact our comprehension, actions, and judgments, often without our consciousness. These prejudices can stem from variables such as race, gender, ethnicity, age, physical appearance, or other characteristics.

This bias takes place when our minds process information grounded on preconceived notions and prior experiences instead of objectively evaluating the situation. This can lead to unfair treatment or discrimination towards individuals or groups without our awareness.

Moreover, unconscious biases are usually deeply embedded in our thinking and conduct, and they can subtly influence our decisions and actions. Recognizing our own unconscious biases and taking measures to alleviate them is crucial to establishing a more comprehensive and equitable society.

It is common to assume that prejudice only exists outside of ourselves and that we are immune to its influence. However, even the most skilled leaders are susceptible to the pervasive effects of prejudice in our world. Factors such as age, gender, religion, or ethnic background can unconsciously shape our perceptions and attitudes toward others.

Consider the case of Jerry, a 35-year-old white Christian man who acted aggressively in the workplace, and Ashmit, a 35-year-old brown Hindu man who was involved in a similar incident. As a leader, it is possible to treat the two individuals differently based on our unconscious biases. Unconscious bias can cause a leader to have a preference for individuals like Jerry or Ashmit, which is known as affinity bias. Additionally, they may also have a conformity bias, where they align with the team's opinion without justification, leading to biased decision-making.

Our personal biases can significantly impact our leadership abilities, which is why it is crucial to assess and eliminate them from our decision-making processes. It is vital to be aware of our biases and their influence on our behavior toward others. This is especially true for leaders who are responsible for guiding and influencing the work of their team members. By recognizing and overcoming our prejudices, we can create an inclusive and equitable workplace that benefits everyone.

Make the "Success in Diversity" Vision a Priority

Making diversity a priority and working towards creating a culture of inclusivity is crucial for any organization. This not only helps create a positive brand image for the company but also improves the productivity of the employees.

Leaders should prioritize the "success in diversity" vision by developing a strategic plan that includes initiatives and programs aimed at promoting diversity and inclusion in the workplace. This includes implementing training programs that address unconscious bias, promoting diversity in hiring practices, and ensuring that all employees feel valued and respected, regardless of their gender, ethnicity, religion, or sexual orientation.

Additionally, leaders should make diversity and inclusion a part of the organization's core values and ensure that it is reflected in every aspect of the company's operations. By doing so, they can attract a diverse talent pool and create an environment where everyone feels comfortable and empowered to share their unique perspectives and ideas.

Prioritizing the "success in diversity" vision is not only the right thing to do, but it is also beneficial for the company's bottom line. Companies that prioritize diversity and inclusivity tend to have a more engaged and motivated workforce, which leads to increased productivity, innovation, and profitability.

Conduct Interactive Meetings to Emphasize the Significance of Having a Shared Identity

To foster a sense of belonging and create a shared identity among employees, leaders should prioritize interactive meetings that highlight commonalities rather than differences. Although it is easy to focus on the things that separate us, it is important to recognize the things that bring us together.

By inviting people from diverse backgrounds to share their ideas in these meetings, leaders can facilitate a deeper understanding and appreciation for each other's perspectives. Moreover, leaders can emphasize the shared goal of working towards the success of the same company, reiterating that everyone is part of the same team.

This sense of belonging can have a positive impact on employees' well-being and performance. When individuals identify more with their role as an employee of the organization rather than their ethnicity, age, or religion, they are more likely to feel valued and motivated.

Leaders can also assign symbols or names to teams to create a sense of belonging and team identity. For example, assigning the title of "champions of peace" to members of Amnesty International can create a strong sense of shared purpose and identity.

In conclusion, leaders should prioritize creating a common identity among employees by organizing interactive meetings that focus on shared values and goals. By emphasizing a shared sense of belonging, leaders can help employees work collaboratively towards achieving organizational success.

Empower Human Resources (HR) to Assist in Resolving Employee Conflict and Improving Industrial Relations

HR empowerment is a critical aspect of an organization's success, and it can go a long way in improving employee engagement and satisfaction. One of the key roles of the human resources department is to help employees resolve conflicts that may arise in the workplace. By empowering HR professionals with the necessary tools and resources, organizations can ensure that their employees receive the support they need to navigate workplace conflicts.

Empowering HR means providing them with the authority and resources they need to take action.

This includes training HR professionals on conflict resolution techniques, providing them with access to mediation and other conflict resolution tools, and giving them the autonomy to make decisions that are in the best interest of the organization and its employees.

When HR professionals are empowered, they can serve as advocates for employees, providing them with a safe space to voice their concerns and grievances. They can also work with managers and supervisors to address conflicts before they escalate, helping to maintain a positive and productive work environment.

In addition to addressing conflicts, empowered HR can also work with employees to identify areas for improvement and implement strategies to enhance employee engagement and retention. This includes conducting regular employee satisfaction surveys, providing career development opportunities, and offering competitive compensation and benefits packages.

Empowering HR is about creating a culture of trust and transparency within an organization. When employees know that HR is there to support them, they are more likely to be engaged and satisfied with their work. This can lead to higher levels of productivity and better business outcomes for the organization as a whole.

In conclusion, empowering HR to help employees resolve conflicts is essential for creating a positive and productive work environment. By investing in HR training, tools, and resources, organizations can ensure that their employees receive the support they need to navigate workplace conflicts and thrive in their roles.

Enhance Collaboration by Incorporating Effective Communication Tools

Effective communication is key to success in any organization. As a leader, it's important to prioritize collaboration and ensure that team members have the necessary tools to communicate effectively. With the rise of remote work, this has become even more crucial since teams may be spread out across different locations and time zones.

There are many communication tools available to help teams collaborate, from email to video conferencing to project management software. It's important to choose the right tools for your team and ensure that everyone is trained to use them effectively.

One tool that can be particularly useful for remote teams is video conferencing. With video conferencing, team members can have face-to-face conversations even if they're in different parts of the world. This can help build stronger relationships among team members and improve collaboration. When using video conferencing, it's important to ensure that everyone has a good internet connection and that there is minimal background noise or distractions.

As my team is spread across the United States, I have been holding virtual meetings twice a week to connect with them personally. During these meetings, which last 15 minutes, we discuss any significant updates or team-related issues. Surveys conducted by the company have indicated that these brief yet regular virtual meetings have strengthened collaboration and trust within the team. Additionally, since the team is remote, it has helped foster a sense of community among us.

Another important tool for collaboration is project management software. This type of software can help teams stay organized and on track with deadlines and tasks. It allows team members to assign tasks to one another, track progress, and communicate about any issues or questions that arise. Some popular project management software options include Trello, Asana, and Basecamp.

Email is also an important communication tool, but it's important to use it effectively. It can be easy for emails to get lost in a cluttered inbox, so it's important to be concise and clear in your messages. It's also helpful to use subject lines that accurately reflect the content of the email and to use bullet points or numbered lists when appropriate.

In addition to these tools, it's important for leaders to foster a culture of open communication. This means encouraging team members to ask questions, share ideas, and provide feedback. It also means being transparent about company goals and challenges. When team members feel like they're part of a shared mission and that their contributions are valued, they're more likely to be motivated and engaged in their work.

Finally, it's important to be mindful of cultural and linguistic differences when communicating with a diverse team. This means being aware of different communication styles and adjusting your own style accordingly. It also means being sensitive to language barriers and making sure that everyone has a clear understanding of what is being communicated.

There is no doubt that effective communication is critical for collaboration and success in any organization. Leaders must prioritize communication tools that are appropriate for their team and foster a culture of open communication. By doing so, they can ensure that their team members are engaged, motivated, and working towards a shared mission.

Celebrate Small Wins in Significant Ways

While the saying "all work and no play makes Jack a dull boy" holds some truth, it is important to note that it also leads to a negative workplace culture and disengaged employees. Leaders who focus solely on work and goals without providing opportunities for fun and enjoyment can create a toxic work environment. This can result in employees showing up to work only for the paycheck and not because they feel a sense of belonging or fulfillment. Meaningful work is essential for creating a positive work environment.

Recognizing and celebrating small wins through events such as parties, dinners, or awards can help employees feel valued and content with their jobs. Fun activities that allow people from different departments to come together and explore their creativity and inner child can also be organized.

This helps foster a positive workplace culture where employees feel connected, engaged, and motivated to contribute to the organization's success.

Promote a Problem-Solving Mentality

As a leader, it may seem like the easiest and most efficient solution to enforce your own ideas and solutions on your team members. However, this approach only provides short-term fixes and fails to empower employees to develop their own problem-solving skills. To truly empower your employees, you need to give them ample space to work through their own conflicts and come up with their own unique solutions.

One effective way to encourage creative problem-solving is to facilitate brainstorming sessions with your team members. By encouraging them to think outside the box, you can help them develop new and innovative ideas for addressing problems. Giving employees the space to come up with their own solutions also fosters a sense of ownership, accountability, and responsibility for their work.

Furthermore, by promoting self-problem-solving behavior, you create an environment where employees can interact with one another more effectively. They can rise above their differences and work collaboratively towards a common goal. This approach creates a more productive and positive work culture where employees feel valued, empowered, and motivated to contribute to the organization's success.

Extend Empathy and Kindness to All Your Team Members

Imagine the scenario where one of your employees approaches you in tears in the middle of an important phone call. As a leader, what would be your initial response? Would you brush them off and continue with your call, or would you put the call on hold and take the time to listen to their concerns? The way you respond can have a significant impact on your relationship with your team.

Empathy is a powerful trait that is often overlooked in leaders. When you take the time to understand your employees' emotions and needs, it makes them feel valued and appreciated. It also shows that you care about their well-being and are willing to support them through difficult times.

Incorporating empathy into your leadership style can have many benefits for your team. Employees are more likely to trust and respect empathetic leaders, and they are more likely to feel motivated and engaged in their work. Likewise, this can lead to a more positive work environment and increased productivity.

Additionally, when leaders demonstrate empathy, they create a culture where employees feel safe and supported. This, in turn, can lead to increased job satisfaction and retention rates. Overall, incorporating empathy into your leadership style is a win-win situation for both you and your team.

Create an Environment of Mutual Respect

Giving respect should not be contingent on whether it is deserved or not; rather, it should be a fundamental principle that is universally applied. An unregulated workplace can breed negative attitudes and even create a toxic environment, which is why it is the responsibility of a leader to establish mutual respect as a non-negotiable value that applies to everyone, irrespective of their role.

Every individual in the organization, from the lowest to the highest level, should be obligated to demonstrate and receive an equal amount of respect. If respect is based on authority or position, it can lead to an unhealthy work environment that is difficult to navigate. To this end, leaders must actively work to foster mutual respect among all employees, regardless of their rank or seniority.

What Happens When Leaders Are Not Collaborative?

When leaders are not collaborative, it can have serious implications for the organization and the people they lead. Leaders who do not value collaboration often create a work environment that is isolated and lacks cross-functional communication. This can result in inefficient processes, duplication of effort, and missed opportunities for innovation and improvement. Collaboration is essential for identifying and addressing challenges that require input and expertise from multiple teams or departments. Without collaboration, problems can go unaddressed, and opportunities for growth and improvement can be missed.

Leaders who are not collaborative may also make decisions without taking into account the perspectives and needs of other stakeholders. This can lead to poor decision-making and resistance from those who feel left out of the decision-making process. A lack of collaboration can create a culture of distrust and disengagement among employees. When people feel that their input is not valued or heard, they may become less motivated and committed to their work. This can result in decreased productivity, lower morale, and higher turnover rates.

The Collaborative Leader

The collaborative leader values teamwork and seeks to bring people together to achieve a common goal. They understand that no one person has all the answers and therefore foster an environment of inclusiveness and open communication. They listen actively to others and value their input, encouraging the sharing of ideas and perspectives.

This leader also prioritizes building relationships and trust within their teams. They understand that a strong foundation of trust allows for open and honest communication, which is essential for effective collaboration. They lead by example and encourage others to do the same, creating a culture of respect and accountability.

In addition, the collaborative leader is adaptable and flexible, able to navigate changing circumstances and pivot as needed. They prioritize learning and growth, seeking out opportunities to improve themselves and their teams. They are also adept at managing conflict, recognizing that differing opinions and perspectives can be valuable when handled constructively.

Overall, the collaborative leader is someone who prioritizes the collective success of the team over individual achievements. They inspire and empower others to work together towards a common purpose, fostering a culture of collaboration and teamwork.

Conclusion

I have touched on the most vital qualities of highly respected leaders throughout this book. However, if I had to emphasize one single trait, it would be emotional intelligence. I believe emotional intelligence is the foundation of most, if not all, the other characteristics. Without it, it would be difficult to manage yourself as a leader, let alone your team. Can you really be collaborative, decisive, confident, adaptable, and more if you don't know how to recognize and manage your own emotions? It is emotional intelligence that enables leaders to understand and manage their own emotions and recognize those of others, leading to better communication, collaboration, and relationship-building skills. It also allows leaders to respond appropriately to challenging situations and manage conflicts effectively, resulting in improved decision-making and overall success.

Moreover, you should always keep in mind that leaders are respected not only for their achievements but also for the way they conduct themselves, their ethics, and their ability to inspire and empower others.

One of the key traits of a highly respected leader is integrity. Ask yourself if you are true to yourself and your values. Remember, highly respected leaders do not pretend to be something they are not or try to please everyone, but they earn respect by being honest, genuine, and consistent.

Another essential trait is empathy, the ability to understand and relate to others' perspectives and emotions. Respected leaders listen to their team members, customers, and stakeholders with an open mind and genuine interest. They create a safe and inclusive environment where people feel valued and heard, and they treat everyone with respect and kindness. Are you this kind of leader? If so, you are certainly doing something right, and you will reap the rewards of creating an engaged and motivated team.

A highly respected leader is also a visionary, someone who has a clear and compelling vision of the future and can inspire others to work towards it. To be this kind of leader, you need to be both strategic and innovative and constantly on the lookout for new opportunities and ways to improve your organization and society. Don't be afraid to take risks but strive to do so after careful consideration and analysis.

Moreover, highly respected leaders are accountable and responsible for their actions and decisions. I don't point this out to be confrontational, but if you're still allowing your team to take the fall for your actions, then you have a long way to go in terms of earning their respect. The golden rule applies here: Do for others what you'd want them to do for you. Be a leader who takes ownership of your mistakes and learns from them. Be a leader who is not too proud to give credit to others for their successes. Lead with integrity and ethics, and do not compromise your values for short-term gains or popularity.

I also spoke about how highly respected leaders empower others. When they do this, they cultivate a growth mindset, a belief that their teams can always learn and improve. They also follow this up with actions to invest in their staff's personal and professional development, offer constructive feedback, and give them enough autonomy to make decisions and tackle challenges on their own. To be this kind of leader, you need to first embrace a growth mindset and view challenges and failures as opportunities for growth. By doing this, you lead your team not just through words but with action. I encourage you to be the leader who creates a culture of continuous learning and improvement. You will never regret taking that stance.

One can hardly talk of efficient leadership without delving into the importance of having excellent communication skills. Efficient leadership demands that leaders convey their messages clearly and persuasively in a way that inspires and motivates others and builds strong relationships. Leaders should be able to adapt their communication style to different audiences and situations and use storytelling, humor, and other techniques to engage and connect with others.

Finally, highly respected leaders are not afraid to collaborate and delegate. They understand that they cannot do everything alone, and they trust and empower their team members to take on responsibilities and contribute to the organization's success. Encouraging teamwork is at the very core of such leadership. By creating a culture of collaboration, they ensure that everyone's ideas and contributions are valued and recognized.

In summary, the secrets of highly respected leaders are a combination of authenticity, empathy, vision, accountability, a growth mindset, communication, and collaboration. These traits can be learned and developed with practice and dedication, and they are essential for any leader who wants to lead with respect, influence, and impact. Highly respected leaders inspire and empower others, create positive change, and leave a lasting legacy.

You Have What It Takes!

As a leader, you have the power to shape your organization, inspire your team, and leave a lasting impact on the world. By developing the traits of highly respected leaders, you can create a culture of excellence that drives success and promotes positive change.

I urge you to take action today to develop these traits. You can start by identifying areas where you can improve and set goals for yourself. Seek out opportunities for growth, such as leadership training programs or mentoring from experienced leaders. Additionally, you can encourage your team to develop these traits as well. The most effective way to do this is by leading by example and providing support and resources for their development. Don't forget to celebrate your team's successes and recognize efforts to build a culture of excellence.

Finally, remember that leadership is a journey and not a destination. Consequently, it takes time, dedication, and hard work to develop the traits of highly respected leaders. However, the rewards are immeasurable, both for you and for those around you. So take that first step today. Commit to developing these traits and becoming the kind of leader that others admire and respect. Your organization, your team, and your world will thank you for it.

References

A quote by Ralph Lauren. (n.d.). Coolnsmart.com. https://www.coolnsmart.com/quote-a-leader-has-the-vision-and-conviction-33352/

Akram, M. (2021, December 23). Best quotes about emotional intelligence and leadership. Peoples Q u o t e s . https://peoplesquotes.com/best-quotes-about-emotional-intelligence-and-leadership

Baker, M. (2019, July 23). Gartner survey shows only half of business leaders feel confident leading their teams today. Gartner. https://www.gartner.com/en/newsroom/press-releases/2019-07-22-gartner-survey-shows-only-half-of-business-leaders-fe

Boskamp, E. (2023, February 16). 35+ compelling workplace collaboration statistics [2023]; The importance of teamwork. Zippia.

https://www.zippia.com/advice/workplace-collaboration-statistics/

Bouchard, J. (2014, August 20). A stupid quotation on leadership from Lao Tzu? LinkedIn. https://www.linkedin.com/pulse/20140820100406-10197807-a-stupid-quotation-on-leadership-from-lao-tzu

Broksic, B. (n.d.). Leaders eat last summary, review, notes.   Growthabit. https://growthabit.com/self-help-books/leaders-eat-last-summary-review-notes/

Chittenden, C. (n.d.). The essence of your leadership.   Talking   About. https://www.talkingabout.com.au/TheEssenceOfYourLeadership

Daskal, L. (n.d.). This is how leaders improve their self   confidence.   Lolly   Daskal. https://www.lollydaskal.com/leadership/this-is-how-leaders-improve-their-self-confidence/

Daskal, L. (n.d.). Why it's important to have decisive leaders.   Lolly   Daskal. https://www.lollydaskal.com/leadership/why-its-important-to-have-decisive-leaders/

Dimovski, A. (2023, March 7). 24+ mesmerizing workplace collaboration statistics [2023] . G o R e m o t e l y . https://goremotely.net/blog/workplace-collaboration/

Emeritus. (2022, July 14). Why emotional intelligence is important in leadership. https://emeritus.org/in/learn/why-emotional-intelligence-is-important-in-leadership/#:~:text=Emotional%20intelligence%20develops%20a%20positive

Espinoza, J. Great leaders are decisive. (n.d.). SIGMA   Assessment   Systems. https://www.sigmaassessmentsystems.com/great-leaders-decisive/#:~:text=In%20the%20workplace%2C%20decisiveness%20is

15 quotes about the importance of integrity as a leader. (2019, November 1). Behavioral Essentials. https://www.behavioralessentials.com/15-quotes-about-the-importance-of-integrity-as-a-leader/#:~:text=%E2%80%9CDon

5 traits of emotionally intelligent leaders. (2022, December   21).   Pluralsight. https://www.pluralsight.com/blog/teams/5-traits-of-an-emotionally-intelligent-leader

Granite State College. (n.d.). Cultivating your leadership capabilities. https://granite.pressbooks.pub/ld820/chapter/9/

Ivy Groupe [@Ivy_Groupe]. (2018, September 7). "No doubt emotional intelligence is more rare than book smarts, but my experience says it is actually more important in the making of a leader. You just can't ignore it." -Jack Welch #emotionalintelligence [Tweet]. Twitter. https://twitter.com/Ivy_Groupe/status/1038152623 646490625

Gupta, P. (2014, September 17). The task of the leader is to get his people from where they are to where they have not been. LinkedIn. https://www.linkedin.com/pulse/20140917151640-37343668-leader-or-an-entrepreneur#:~:text=%E 2%80%9CThe%20task%20of%20the%20leader

Harvard Business Review. (2004, January). Leading by feel. https://hbr.org/2004/01/leading-by-feel

How successful leaders use empowerment to build trust and excellence. (n.d.). David Huntoon. http://www.davidhuntoon.com/leaders/successful-leaders-use-empowerment-build-trust-excellence /

How to build your leadership vision. (n.d.). Tony Robbins. https://www.tonyrobbins.com/what-is-leadership/leadership-vision/

Jouany, V., & Martic, K. (2023, January 1). 18 leadership communication trends to look for in 2022. Haiilo. https://haiilo.com/blog/18-leadership-communication-trends-to-look-for-in-2020/

Klaussen, K. (2020, September 4). Why is integrity important in leadership? Babson Thought & Action. https://entrepreneurship.babson.edu/why-is-integrity-important-in-leadership/

LaMarco, N. (2018, December 3). The concept of empowerment in leadership. Chron. https://smallbusiness.chron.com/concept-empowerment-leadership-15371.html

Leading Effectively Staff. (2021, August 24). Adapting to change requires flexible leadership. Center for Creative Leadership. https://www.ccl.org/articles/leading-effectively-articles/adaptability-1-idea-3-facts-5-tips/#:~:text=Adaptability%20is%20a%20requirement

Leading Effectively Staff. (2023, January 27). 15 tips for effective communication in leadership. Center for Creative Leadership. https://www.ccl.org/articles/leading-effectively-art icles/communication-1-idea-3-facts-5-tips/

Lee, A., Willis, S., & Tian, A. W. (2018, March 2). When empowering employees works, and when it doesn't. Harvard Business Review. https://hbr.org/2018/03/when-empowering-emplo yees-works-and-when-it-doesnt

Michael. (n.d.). 30 best vision quotes. Leadership Geeks. https://www.leadershipgeeks.com/vision-quotes/

Nadler, R. (n.d.). Great leaders have integrity. SIGMA Assessment Systems. https://www.sigmaassessmentsystems.com/integrit y-in-leaders/#:~:text=Integrity%20in%20leaders% 20refers%20to

Peeps HR. (2019, July 8). The impact of poor communication in the workplace. https://www.peepshr.co.uk/resource-centre/the-i mpact-of-poor-communication-in-the-workplace /#:~:text=There%20is%20the%20opportunity%20f or

Reddy, K. (n.d.). Why confidence is important for a leader? 18 best reasons. Wisestep https://content.wisestep.com/why-confidence-is-important-for-a-leader-best-reasons/

Shelton, S. (n.d.). The best leaders empower others. Executive Leadership Consulting. https://executiveleader.com/leader-empowerment/

Sisodia, R., & Gelb, M. (2019, September 17). The healing organization: Awakening the conscience of business to help save the world. HarperCollins Leadership.

Stark, P. (2014, October 7). The critical connection between confidence and leadership. LinkedIn. https://www.linkedin.com/pulse/20141007145901-24517615-the-critical-connection-between-confidence-and-leadership/

Sudbrink, L. (n.d.). Emotional intelligence is an important part of strong leadership. Business Leadership Today. https://businessleadershiptoday.com/emotional-intelligence-is-an-important-part-of-strong-leadership/

The Vibe Team. (2022, May 5). 35 quotes about communication for inspiring team collaboration. Vibe. https://vibe.us/blog/35-quotes-about-communication/

Todorovic, J. (n.d.). 7 principles for achieving leadership integrity. RLX Business Solutions. https://relax.ph/blog/leadership-integrity/

What is decision making? (2023, March 13). McKinsey & Company. https://www.mckinsey.com/featured-insights/mckinsey-explainers/what-is-decision-making

Why a decisive leader is a more successful leader. (2021, January 18). Practice Business. https://practicebusiness.co.uk/why-a-decisive-leader-is-a-more-successful-leader

Why adaptability is a critical capability for future leadership. (2020, November 9). Gateley. https://gateleyplc.com/insight/quick-reads/why-adaptability-is-a-critical-capability-for-future-leadership/

Why effective leadership starts with communication. (n.d.). Eagle's Flight.

https://www.eaglesflight.com/resource/why-effecti
ve-leadership-starts-with-communication/

Why self-confidence is vital for leaders. (2021, May
20).   Strammer.
https://strammer.com/en/why-self-confidence-is-
vital-for-leaders/

Ziegler, P. (2022-a, November 22). How can
exceptional leaders bring diverse people together?
Best   Diplomats.
https://bestdiplomats.org/how-leaders-can-bring-
people-together/

Ziegler, P. (2022-b, December 2). Significance of
collaborative leadership in a digital era. Best
D   i   p   l   o   m   a   t   s   .
https://bestdiplomats.org/collaborative-leadership
/#:~:text=Collaborative%20leadership%20provide
s%20an%20environment

Zmorenski, D. (n.d.). Why leaders must have vision.
Noria   Corporation.
https://www.reliableplant.com/Read/29109/leader
s-have-vision

About the Author

 Jeffrey Harvey's over 25 years as a professional engineer in STEM positions grants him unique expertise to answer questions young STEM professionals face. The STEM field is ever-growing, and the need for professionals has never been higher, so helping a whole new generation succeed has become one of Jeffrey's driving forces. As a father to three boys—all with STEM-related fields of study and work—and as a professional himself, he understands the struggles this new wave of young professionals face.

Originally from Wyoming, Jeffrey now resides in Oklahoma with his lovely wife, two foreign exchange students, and their Basenji dog. In his downtime, he enjoys being outdoors, writing books, remodeling, reading, traveling, and learning about other cultures. His extensive experience in different leadership positions, including Engineering Director, several positions as an Engineering Manager, accounting-related supervisor, Project Manager for major and minor projects leading all disciplines, and different individual contributor engineering and STEM roles for two Fortune 500 companies, make him a multi-faceted expert that can help any professional achieve their dreams.

JeffreyHarveyPE.com

Also By

STEM Secrets for Interviewing

Unlock the secrets to acing your STEM interviews
with "*STEM Secrets for Interviewing*." This
comprehensive guide is designed to equip you with
the essential strategies and insider knowledge you
need to confidently navigate the challenging world
of STEM interviews. Whether you're a recent

graduate, a seasoned professional, or transitioning into a new field, this book provides invaluable tips on how to showcase your skills, present your accomplishments, and stand out among other candidates. With expert advice and real-life examples, "STEM Secrets for Interviewing" will help you secure the job of your dreams and launch a successful career in the exciting realm of STEM.

STEM Secrets When Success is the Only Option

In the fiercely competitive landscape of STEM fields, success is not just an option—it's a necessity. "STEM Secrets When Success is the Only Option" unveils the winning strategies and mindset that propel individuals to extraordinary heights in their STEM careers. This book delves into the mindsets, habits, and approaches of highly accomplished professionals, offering invaluable guidance on goal setting, overcoming obstacles, and maintaining resilience in the face of adversity. Packed with inspiring stories and practical advice, this must-read resource will empower you to unleash your full potential, achieve unparalleled success, and become a true trailblazer in your chosen STEM field.

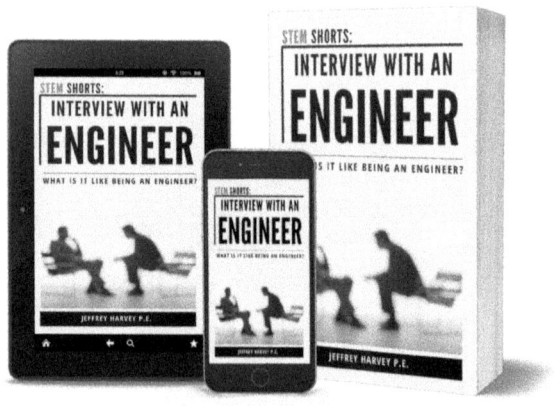

STEM SHORTS: Interview with an Engineer

Ever wondered what it's like to walk in the shoes of a successful engineer? "STEM Short Interview with an Engineer" takes you on a captivating journey through the experiences, insights, and wisdom of a seasoned engineer. This engaging book presents a collection of thought-provoking interviews, offering a rare glimpse into the fascinating world of STEM from the perspective of an accomplished professional. With a blend of personal anecdotes, career advice, and industry trends, this concise and informative read provides aspiring engineers with invaluable guidance for their own journeys. Whether you're a student exploring your career options or a professional seeking inspiration, "STEM Short Interview with an Engineer" is an illuminating resource that will broaden your horizons and fuel your passion for the field.

or visit

https://jeffreyharveype.com/books/

"Help others discover success!

Share your review to mentor others"

Dear Reader,
Thank you sincerely for reading my book. Your support means the world to me, and I am immensely grateful. I hope you enjoyed the book and found it worthwhile. Your reviews are highly valued as they provide valuable insights for improvement. I carefully read each review to gain valuable insights. Thank you for helping make this book a success.

With heartfelt appreciation,

Jeffrey Harvey